"UNWRAPPING" the STANDARDS

A Simple Process to Make Standards *Manageable*

LARRY AINSWORTH

LEAD+
LEARN
PRESS

Englewood, CO

LEAD+
LEARN
PRESS

Lead + Learn Press
317 Inverness Way South, Suite 150
Englewood, CO 80112
Phone (866) 399-6019 • Fax (303) 504-9417
www.LeadandLearn.com

Editor: Allison Wedell Schumacher

Library of Congress Cataloging-in-Publication Data:

Ainsworth, Larry.
   "Unwrapping" the standards : a simple process to make standards manageable / Larry Ainsworth;
      p.   cm.
Includes bibliographical references and index.
   ISBN 978-0-9709455-5-6
   1. Education—Standards—United States.   I. Title.
   LB3060.83.A39 2003
   379.1'58'0973—dc21

                                                                    2003043677

Printed in the United States of America

10 09 08   07 08 09 10

"UNWRAPPING" the STANDARDS

A Simple Process to Make Standards *Manageable*

Other Titles by Larry Ainsworth

Common Formative Assessments; How to Connect Standards-Based Instruction and Assessment

Five Easy Steps to a Balanced Math Program, Second Edition (Primary, Upper Elementary, and Secondary)

Power Standards: Identifying the Standards that Matter the Most

Student-Generated Rubrics: An Assessment Model to Help All Students Succeed

Dedication

I respectfully dedicate this book to Dr. Donald J. Viegut, Director of Pre K-12 Curriculum and Instruction, Merrill Area Public Schools, Merrill, Wisconsin, and to Dr. Ronald Herring, Executive Director of the California International Studies Project, based at Stanford University in Palo Alto, California.

Dr. Donald J. Viegut first introduced me to the concept of "unwrapping" the standards when I visited his school district in the fall of 1999. Little did I realize at that time the far-reaching impact this meeting would have on my work to improve education in school systems across the nation. I am deeply indebted to him.

Dr. Ronald Herring continually challenged me to take the practice of designing standards-based performance assessments to higher levels of effectiveness. In addition to being the first to recommend that I include the "unwrapping" process as part of performance assessment design, he helped me deepen my own personal understanding of Big Ideas and Essential Questions and the roles they play in performance assessments. By assisting me, he has indirectly helped educators nationwide. The success of this constantly evolving and improving process is in great measure owed to the insightful questions and suggestions of Dr. Herring.

Special Acknowledgment

I wish to particularly acknowledge the exceptional contributions to the fields of curriculum and assessment by Grant Wiggins and Jay McTighe. Among their significant body of work, *Understanding by Design*, published by the Association for Supervision and Curriculum and Development (ASCD), is a landmark achievement and has influenced thinkers, writers, and practitioners throughout the world. It has been my good fortune to work with a number of educators who use the ideas and structure of *Understanding by Design*, and thus the work of Wiggins and McTighe has had a profound influence on the process described in my book. I have sought in these pages to complement their ideas, drawing from my own perspective as a practitioner and seeking to offer educators practical help in dealing with these very complex issues. While I gratefully acknowledge their contribution and that of many other authors to my developing understanding of educational theory and practice, I accept responsibility for and regret any unintentional errors and omissions.

Acknowledgments

This book reflects the cumulative insights of literally thousands of educators across the United States with whom I have had the opportunity to share these ideas. To all of these educators, I wish to express my appreciation and gratitude for contributing to what I consider to be the collective wisdom of the "unwrapping" standards process.

First and foremost, I must thank the two educators to whom this book is dedicated, Dr. Donald J. Viegut of the Merrill Area Public Schools in Merrill, Wisconsin, and Dr. Ronald Herring of the California International Studies Project.

I also wish to thank the coordinators of the national, state, and regional conferences and educational organizations that have invited me to share these methods with their participants. These include: the U.S. Department of Education, the New York Department of Education, the Ohio Department of Education, Indiana ASCD, Indiana Computer Educators' Conference, the Southern Regional Education Board in Georgia, Harvard University's Graduate School of Education Principals' Center in Massachusetts, the College of William and Mary STARS Conference in Virginia, the Claremont Graduate School of Education in California, the California International Studies Project, the Ventura Country Office of Education in California, the Miami Valley Leadership Academy in Montgomery County, Ohio, and the Ohio Educational Association.

My sincere gratitude and appreciation extend to the California International Studies Project administrators, staff, and site directors: Dr. Ron Herring, Joan Benton, Chalyn Newman, Marianne Loeser, Kent Safford, Marilyn Benefiel, Connie DeCapite, Jonathan Weil, Teresa Hudock, Jackie Purdy, Sandy Shepard, Dianne Bruckner, and Maggie DeLeon, along with their assistants and the educators they support. Each of them has offered invaluable insights and contributions to this work.

Special thanks go to Connie DeCapite of California State University at Fullerton, California; Jane Cimolino of Snohomish, Washington; Gary Colburn of Fresno Unified School District in Fresno, California; Sue Sims of Vista Unified School District in Vista, California; Curt Greeley and Chris Grisaffi of the Santa Maria Joint Union High School District in Santa Maria, California; and Will Sibley of the Metropolitan School District of Wayne Township, Indianapolis, Indiana, for contributing commentaries that support this process or sharing how these practices have significantly improved their professional practices. My thanks also go to the secondary educators and literacy coaches of Lawrence Township in Indianapolis, Indiana, for their valued input in determining the subtitle of this book!

I wish to particularly acknowledge and thank the following schools and school systems that have participated in and contributed to the practice of "unwrapping" the standards. I have listed these according to states. I hope I have not excluded anyone, and if so, please accept my apologies!

In **California,** these include: Los Angeles Unified School District K administrators; Belmont High School math and science departments in Los Angeles; Phil Gore and the Ventura County Superintendent of Schools Office; Cajon Valley Unified in El Cajon; Hoover High School in San Diego; Carr Middle School and Martin Luther King, Jr. Elementary School in Santa Ana; Edgewood Middle School in Covina; Anaheim Union High School District; Bear Creek High School in Lodi Unified; Fresno Unified; Manteca Unified; Tracy Unified; educators from Chico area schools; Lennox Middle School in Lennox; Palm Springs Unified; Rialto Unified School District administrators; Santa Maria Joint Union High School District; Stockton Unified; and the Washington Unified School District in West Sacramento. Special thanks also to the administrators and educators of Newark Unified School District in Newark, California, who so enthusiastically supported the Center's performance assessment model *prior to* my development of the "unwrapping" process.

In **Georgia,** the Muscogee County School District in Columbus; in **Indiana,** the Evansville-Vanderburgh School Corporation, Hamilton Southeastern Schools, Lawrence Township Plainfield School Corporation, and Wayne Township; in **New Jersey,** Trenton Unified; in **New York,** the New York City School; in **Ohio,** the school districts of Centerville, Dayton, Huber Heights, Kettering, Miamisburg, New Lebanon, Northmont, Oakwood, West Carrollton, the Educational Service Center of the Miami Valley Leadership Academy in Montgomery County, Princeton Schools in Sharonville, Tri County ESC, and Van Wert Schools in Van Wert; in **Oklahoma,** the Oklahoma City Schools administrators; in **Virginia,** Norfolk Public Schools and Virginia Beach City Public Schools; and in **Wisconsin,** Merrill Area Public Schools and the School District of Waukesha in partnership with Alverno College, especially professor Suzann Gardner. Thanks also to the administrators and educators of all the other Wisconsin districts with whom I had the privilege to share the Center's performance assessment model *prior to* my development of the "unwrapping" process. These include: Gillett, Green Bay, New London, Portage, and Tomahawk.

To my colleagues at The Leadership and Learning Center (formerly the Center for Performance Assessment) who assisted in and/or supported the publication of this work, my sincere thanks go to Dr. Douglas B. Reeves, Sarah Abrahamson, Eileen Allison, Greg Atkins, Ken Bingenheimer, Nan Caldwell, Laura Davis, Anne Fenske, Tony Flach, Angie Hodapp, Paul Kane, Michelle LePatner, Matt Minney, Janelle Miller, Bernadette Reynolds, Stacy Scott, Devon Sheldon, Jill Unzicker-Lewis, Mike White, and Katherine Woodson. I extend special thanks once again to my editor, Allison Wedell Schumacher and Angie Hodapp, project coordinator, for readying this material for publication.

To my wife, Candy, for her patience, love, and continuous support throughout this entire process.

Lastly, I wish to express my sincere gratitude to all the educators, administrators, and curriculum leaders who have so generously contributed their "unwrapped" standards with accompanying Big Ideas and Essential Questions for the publication of this work. Educators everywhere will have a better idea of how to "unwrap" their own standards as a direct result of your examples.

About the Author

Larry Ainsworth is the Executive Director of Professional Development at The Leadership and Learning Center (formerly the Center for Performance Assessment) in Englewood, Colorado. He travels widely throughout the United States to assist school systems in implementing standards and standards-based performance assessments in the K-12 classroom. He also leads seminars in Data-Driven Decision Making as well as seminars based on the two books he co-authored with Jan Christinson, *Student Generated Rubrics: An Assessment Model to Help All Students Succeed,* and *Five Easy Steps to a Balanced Math Program.* Larry's primary motivation is to assist educators in helping all students succeed, by taking the mystery out of the instruction, learning, and assessment process.

Larry has delivered keynote addresses nationwide, most notably for the U.S. Department of Education, New York Department of Education, Ohio Department of Education, Michigan Department of Education, Harvard University Graduate School of Education's Principals' Center, Indiana Association for Supervision and Curriculum Development (ASCD), California ASCD, Virginia Title I and STARS conferences, and the Southern Regional Education Board. He has conducted breakout sessions at national and regional conferences throughout the country, including the California Math Council, the California International Studies Project, the Alabama CLAS Summer Institute, the Delaware Professional Development Conference, the National Council of Teachers of Mathematics, the national ASCD conference, and the National School Conference Institute.

With 24 years of experience as an upper-elementary and middle school classroom educator in demographically diverse schools, Larry brings a varied background and wide range of professional experiences to each of his presentations. He has held numerous leadership roles within school districts, including mentor teacher and K-12 math committee co-chair, and has served as a mathematics assessment consultant in several San Diego County school districts.

In addition to continuing his full-time presentation schedule and writing *"Unwrapping the Standards,* Larry has authored *Power Standards: Identifying the Standards that Matter the Most.*

Larry holds a Master of Science degree in educational administration.

Contents

Detailed Contents

Chapter Nine
"Unwrapping" the Standards—The Step-by-Step Process 207

Chapter Ten
From "Unwrapping" Standards to Performance Assessments 211

Appendix A
"Unwrapping" Standards Template 214

Appendix B
Bloom's *Taxonomy* 219

Introduction

Today's educators in all grades and subject areas are striving to ensure that their students meet the academic content standards now driving instruction and assessment throughout the nation.

Standards—unlike so many passing trends in education—are here to stay. All 50 states (Iowa has determined standards at the local level) and Washington, D.C., have formally established academic content standards that specify what students are expected to know and be able to do at each grade level in the various content areas. The federal reauthorization of the Elementary and Secondary Education Act of 2001—"No Child Left Behind"—now requires that *all* students demonstrate proficiency in reading and math as measured on state assessments by the end of the 2013-14 school year. States are to begin testing students in reading and math by the end of the 2005-06 school year. Schools will have to meet their AYP ("adequate yearly progress") performance targets, not only for the student population as a whole but also for various subgroups: students from racial and ethnic minorities, students with disabilities, students who are economically disadvantaged, and those with limited English proficiency (2002). This requirement is placing enormous accountability pressure on everyone involved. Because these high-stakes assessments are to be aligned with state standards, the standards have naturally become the critical focus for achieving the results that schools are expected to produce. To meet these rigorous demands, our educators need practical strategies, not only to realize higher student achievement levels in reading and mathematics, but also in every other content area.

The process of "unwrapping" the standards is a simple yet powerful practice to accomplish a more effective implementation of the standards with a corresponding improvement of student performance on *all* assessment measures.

Overview and Endorsements

"Unwrapping" the academic content standards is a proven technique to help educators identify from the full text of the standards exactly what they need to teach their students. "Unwrapped" standards provide clarity as to what students must know and be able to do. When teachers take the time to analyze each standard and identify its essential concepts and skills, the result is more effective instructional planning, assessment, and student learning. From the "unwrapped" concepts and skills, educators next determine the "Big Ideas," or learning goals, that they want their students to remember long after instruction ends, and then write "Essential Questions" to guide their students toward the attainment of these Big Ideas.

In the "unwrapping" standards seminars I have conducted over the last three years for The Leadership and Learning Center (formerly the Center for Performance Assessment), both new and experienced educators nation-wide have wholeheartedly endorsed this in-depth look at the standards. Many have said that it is the most powerful tool they have yet seen for managing the standards effectively. The great news is that this process works equally well in every grade level, in every subject matter area, and with every state's standards.

One of my favorite endorsements of the "unwrapping" process came from an educator in a western state. After completing the first day of the "unwrapping" seminar, he stood up and made a startling admission to the other 60 or more educators present.

"Hi, everyone, my name is _____, and I have a confession to make. Although I've been teaching for several years, today is the first time I've ever *really* looked at the standards. At last I feel I understand what it is I'm supposed to be teaching my students."

The audience broke into empathetic laughter and applause.

Some months later, another seminar participant announced that not only did he now understand better what he was supposed to teach, but that he had just gotten the idea to post in his classroom the "unwrapped" standards in *student-friendly language* so that his students would also understand clearly what their learning targets were.

Others have taken that idea one step further by sharing the "unwrapped" version of the standards with parents to help them better understand—in simpler language—exactly what their children will be expected to learn.

The process you are about to learn is practical, it can be understood quickly, and perhaps best of all, it can be implemented immediately to improve both the quality of instruction and the achievement of all students.

Just Good Teaching

Even though the process was developed in response to the need for a more effective way to manage the standards, essentially this is about *good teaching*. Experienced educators have told me that this technique formalizes what they have been doing informally throughout their careers: deciding what is important for students to learn in a particular content area ("unwrapping"), helping students make connections to other areas of study and utilize higher-level thinking skills (Big Ideas), and engaging students in the material to be studied by setting a purpose for learning (Essential Questions). Take away the standards and the state tests, and educators would still utilize these methods because they are practical and because they work!

How It All Began

I first heard the term "unwrapping" the standards in the fall of 1999 from Dr. Don Viegut, Director of Pre K-12 Curriculum and Instruction in Merrill, Wisconsin. Under the leadership of Dr. Viegut, district educators worked collaboratively to "unwrap" Wisconsin academic content standards in order to pinpoint what the standards specified students needed to learn and be able to do. During my visit, Dr. Viegut and principal Karen Heldt explained how the "unwrapping" process greatly assisted Merrill teachers in planning instruction and assessment. Intrigued by the potential of this practice to improve student achievement, I began to further develop these ideas in my own work with educators.

I introduced "unwrapping" the standards in the spring of 2000 at a performance assessment seminar in Burlingame, California, sponsored by the California International Studies Project, one of several statewide subject matter projects. The educators in attendance worked through the different steps of the process and immediately recognized its value. Over the next two years, I continued to refine these ideas with valuable input and feedback from K-12 educators who participated in numerous CISP workshops across the state.

In June of 2000, I introduced the technique of "unwrapping" the standards at The Leadership and Learning Center summer professional development academy in Denver, Colorado. This was a four-day advanced seminar for participants who had already learned how to design a standards-based performance assessment and were returning to further refine their understanding of the process. Educators in attendance commented that the "unwrapping" process enabled them to design much more effective *standards-based* performance tasks because they were now able to focus on the specific concepts and skills *within* the standards.

Since that time, I have continued to incorporate the valued suggestions and insights I have received from educators all over the United States. One of the reasons this process continues to be embraced so enthusiastically by everyone is because it truly reflects the "collective wisdom" of all those K-12 educators with whom I have had the great fortune to collaborate.

Organization of the Book

The book is designed to be a practical manual that will guide the reader step-by-step through each part of the "unwrapping" standards process. It will serve as a useful reference to educators who have already learned the process in The Leadership and Learning Center seminars and wish to further refine their own understanding. It will also provide educators with an excellent way of introducing their colleagues to the process and working through it together.

Chapter One provides a detailed explanation of how to "unwrap" the standards to identify the important concepts and skills contained within them and then arrange those concepts and skills on a graphic organizer. Five representative examples of "unwrapped" standards from the primary, upper elementary, middle, and high school grade spans in four different content areas will illustrate how to do this.

Once the standards have been "unwrapped" and a graphic organizer has been created, the next step is to identify the Big Ideas, or lasting understandings, embedded within these concepts and skills that educators want students to realize and remember long after instruction ends. Chapter Two presents the rationale and process for identifying the Big Ideas.

The final step in the process is to write Essential Questions that educators will share with students at the inception of an instructional unit. These questions are used as "instructional filters" to select lessons and activities that will advance student understanding of the "unwrapped" concepts and skills and ultimately lead students to discover the Big Ideas *on their own*. The final goal is for students to be able to answer the Essential Questions with the Big Ideas, *stated in their own words,* by the conclusion of an instructional unit. Chapter Three offers the rationale and process for writing the Essential Questions and using them to guide instruction and assessment.

Chapter Four presents proven ways for "working smarter, not harder" by describing how to involve *all* educators in a particular school and/or district in the "unwrapping" standards process.

Chapters Five through Eight are each written specifically for a different grade span—primary, upper elementary, middle school, and high school—to provide readers with a veritable "bank" of "unwrapped" standards, Big Ideas, and Essential Questions from different content areas that they can refer to as they work through the "unwrapping" process alone and with their colleagues. Owing to the contributions of K-12 educators across the country who generously shared their work for the publication of this book, over 80 examples of "unwrapped" standards from a variety of different content areas have been included.

Chapter Nine reviews how to "unwrap" standards in a concise, step-by-step, checklist format. This checklist can serve as an easy reference for groups of educators as they work through their own "unwrapping" process.

Chapter Ten briefly addresses how educators can use "unwrapping," either as a stand-alone practice to better focus instruction and assessment for *any* unit of instruction, or as a foundation for developing a unit around a related collection of standards-based performance assessment tasks.

In the Appendices Section, readers will find two documents: The Leadership and Learning Center "Unwrapping" Template that I developed for use by educators as they "unwrap" their own state standards in their particular content areas; and a summary of Bloom's *Taxonomy* to reference when prioritizing the "unwrapped" skills according to a higher-order thinking skills hierarchy and/or developing their Big Ideas and Essential Questions.

Intellectual understanding ripens into experiential understanding whenever there is the opportunity to *apply* immediately new ideas learned. Toward this end, I have included at the end of selected chapters a Reader's Assignment to assist readers in "unwrapping" their own self-selected standards while reading the information.

"Unwrapping" the Standards will benefit classroom teachers, school and district administrators, curriculum coordinators, and instructional specialists in all grade levels and content areas. It will assist them in improving achievement for *all* students by focusing on the concepts and skills students need for success. The straightforward and easy-to-read format of the book, along with the wealth of examples of "unwrapped" standards, will enable readers to understand and then confidently apply this simple, proven technique for making the standards *manageable!*

CHAPTER ONE

"Unwrapping" the Standards

Definitions

Let's begin with a more detailed definition of what "unwrapping" actually means. "Unwrapping" the standards means to identify the concepts and skills found in both the ***standards*** (the *general* statements of learning outcomes—what students need to know and be able to do) and the ***indicators*** (the *grade-specific* learning outcomes). It means to examine the standards and the grade-specific indicators listed beneath them to determine exactly what students need to (1) ***know*** (the concepts or content) and (2) ***be able to do*** (the skills) through a (3) ***particular context*** (what educators will use to teach students the concepts and skills).

Concepts can be defined as abstract ideas that point to a larger set of understandings, (e.g., peace, democracy, culture, change, patterns, power, etc.). ***Content*** refers to the specific information students need to know in a given standard, its related indicators, or in an entire course of study. Often educators use these terms interchangeably when they are "unwrapping" standards.

To simplify the definitions, think of the **concepts** or content as being *the important **nouns** and noun phrases* embedded in the standards and indicators, and the **skills** as being *the **verbs***. When an educator "unwraps" a standard, s/he is looking for the important nouns and verbs students need to know and be able to do.

Grade-Span Examples

To illustrate the "unwrapping" process in the first three chapters, I have selected standards from the four grade spans (K-2, 3-5, 6-8, and 9-12) in four content areas: lower elementary math, upper elementary science, middle school history/social science, and high school language arts. There are five examples of "unwrapped" standards in all since I included both a writing example and a reading example for high school language arts.

In Chapter Two, I will describe how to look at these same "unwrapped" standards and determine the Big Ideas found within them. Then, in Chapter Three, I will explain how to write Essential Questions matched to the Big Ideas for these same "unwrapped" standards. By using the same "unwrapped" standards examples in all three chapters, the reader will see how the whole process is developed step-by-step.

Select Your Standards to Unwrap

Whether working alone or with grade-level or department colleagues, the first "unwrapping" step is to select one particular grade in one content area of the curriculum. Look over the standards and grade-specific indicators listed underneath and decide which ones you wish to "unwrap."

The first question that arises in our seminars is always, "How many standards and indicators should we choose?"

Let's keep it simple at first. Choose one standard and its related indicators with which you are familiar and "unwrap" those. After you become comfortable with the process, you can select more than one standard and related indicators and collectively "unwrap" them all. Ultimately, educators "unwrap" the specific standards and indicators targeted for an instructional unit.

Underline Nouns, Circle Verbs

The next step is to carefully read through your selected standard and related indicators, and as you do so, **underline** the key *concepts* (important nouns and noun phrases) and **circle** the *skills* (the verbs). Remember, the concepts are what the students must know, and the skills or performance verbs are what they must be able to do. If a particular verb appears in its "-ing" form, and it is clearly a skill students need to be able to do, circle it as is. In the next step of the process, you can list it in its root form, if you prefer.

I often observe educators in our seminars using two different-colored highlighters or pens, highlighting the concepts in one color and the skills in another. Visually, this can be a more useful way to distinguish between concepts and skills.

Create a Graphic Organizer

Now you are ready to create a graphic organizer that represents the standard and its related indicators in their "unwrapped" state. Whether you prefer to outline, create a bulleted list, or create a concept-map (described below), the next step in the process is to organize the identified concepts and skills in a way that makes the most sense to you. You can thus capture from the wording of the standards and indicators the concepts and skills students need to learn, and list them so that they stand out in "high relief." If you do the process thoroughly, you will be able to set aside the standards documents in complete confidence, knowing you have represented on your graphic organizer everything students need to know and be able to do with regard to that particular standard and its indicators.

In the examples that follow, I have represented each concept and skill on the graphic organizer in substantially the same words as they appear in the standards and indicators. I have also endeavored to list them in the same order. Educators are certainly at liberty to summarize, cluster, or abbreviate certain concepts and skills when they create their own graphic organizer. What is *essential* is that the graphic organizer accurately represents the full list of what students need to know and be able to do relative to the standard(s) and indicator(s) in focus.

How to **organize the nouns** you have underlined? Standards in certain states and grade levels organize the standards and indicators under major headings. Those same major headings can be written on the graphic organizer, and each "unwrapped" concept can then be listed beneath its appropriate heading. This makes organizing the concepts fairly easy to do. But if such major headings do not appear in the standards, simply list down the left side of a sheet of paper all the underlined concepts in the same order they appear in the standards text. Then group all the related concepts together, determine your own headings, and list the related concepts beneath them. This is very much like outlining a passage of text where you either copy on paper the evident major headings under which to list the underlined concepts or decide your own headings if they are not provided. Often educators ask themselves during this step of the "unwrapping" process, "What are the *major* concepts under which I can 'plug in' all the minor ones?" These suggestions for organizing the concepts will be illustrated in the forthcoming examples.

How to **organize the skills?** Usually the skills are simply listed in the same order in which they appear in the standards and indicators. Educators have found it very helpful to write the "target" of the skill parenthetically after it. The "target" is the concept (noun or noun phrase) that the student must apply through a particular skill (verb). An example of this would be "identify (cause and effect)" where the targeted concept "cause and effect" is applied through the skill "identify." This pairing of skills with concept targets is described in more detail later in the chapter, as is the use of Bloom's *Taxonomy* (1956) for listing the skills in higher-order thinking skills ascendancy.

If you prefer to create a concept map (also known as a "mind map"), where you write the major concept headings in circles or ovals and list the related concepts on lines drawn out from those shapes, you may be interested in visiting the website *www.inspiration.com*. They offer a graphic organizer software program that educators are using to map text but that can also be utilized to represent "unwrapped" standards in a concept map format.

Deciding Topics or Context

The *Topics or Context* section of the organizer refers to the specific lessons, activities, or units of instruction classroom educators will use to teach their students the concepts and skills contained in the "unwrapped" standard(s) and indicators. This is where educators can "personalize" the graphic organizer by being as general or specific as they choose in determining what instructional materials, lessons, activities, and text chapters they will utilize in their own programs. The topics or context may be decided as the graphic organizer is developed or determined later, after the Big Ideas and Essential Questions have been written and instructional planning begins.

Examples of "Unwrapped" Standards with Commentary

Here is how I "unwrapped" standards and indicators in four different content areas in the four grade spans. State standards documents do not typically provide the labels "standard" and "indicator" before each standard and indicator. I have taken the liberty of adding these labels in the following illustrations for the sake of clarity. Notice that I have CAPITALIZED the skills (verbs) when I typed them rather than circling or highlighting them as educators do when using hard copies of the standards text.

Note: I have deliberately not identified in the text the states from which these standards and indicators appear, in order to keep the focus on the *process* of how to "unwrap" the standards rather than on the unique content of any one particular state's documents. In the References section at the end of the book, I have identified the state and national locations from which these standards and indicators were excerpted.

I recommend reading through each of the examples below even though secondary educators will naturally prefer looking only at secondary examples rather than elementary examples, and vice versa. The commentary I provide with each one will collectively describe the "unwrapping" process in full and answer many of the questions that are sure to arise as you work through the process later on your own.

FIRST EXAMPLE
Grade 2 Mathematics Standard
Number Computation

Standard: **Students USE <u>numerical</u> and <u>computational</u> <u>concepts</u> and <u>procedures</u> in a variety of situations.**

Indicator: **Number Sense** — The student DEMONSTRATES <u>number sense</u> for <u>three-digit whole numbers</u> and <u>simple fractions</u> in a variety of situations.

Indicator: **Number Systems and Their Properties**—The student DEMONSTRATES an understanding of <u>simple fractions</u> (<u>fourths</u>, <u>thirds</u>, <u>halves</u>) and <u>three-digit whole numbers</u> with a special emphasis on <u>place value</u>, and RECOGNIZES, APPLIES, and EXPLAINS their <u>properties</u>.

Indicator: **Estimation**—The student APPLIES <u>numerical estimation</u> with <u>whole numbers up to 999</u>, <u>simple fractions</u>, and <u>money</u>.

Notice that under the bolded standard, which states in *general* terms what students need to know and be able to do, there are three major indicators (*specific* number computation learning outcomes for second-grade students). The concepts (important nouns) have been underlined, and the skills (verbs) have been capitalized. Each of the three indicators begins with a bolded label. These labels will serve as major headings on the graphic organizer. Each underlined concept can then be listed beneath its appropriate label, or beneath several labels if repeated.

Major headings are not always apparent in the standards documents. In this particular example, it seemed logical to use the three labels provided in the indicators as the major concept headings on the graphic organizer. In the remaining examples, I will offer suggestions for identifying these major headings when they are not self-evident.

See how I organized my "unwrapped" concepts and skills below, remembering that your own graphic organizer can be created in whatever format works best for you.

Graphic Organizer
"Unwrapping" Number Computation Standard Grade 2

Concepts: ***Need to <u>Know</u> About <u>Number Computation</u>***

Number Sense
- Three-digit whole numbers
- Simple fractions

Number Systems and Their Properties
- Simple fractions (fourths, thirds, halves)
- Three-digit whole numbers
- Place value
- Properties

Estimation
- Numerical estimation
- Whole numbers to 999
- Simple fractions
- Money

Skills: ***Be Able to <u>Do</u>***
- Use (numerical/computational concepts and procedures)
- Demonstrate (number sense, simple fractions, 3-digit whole numbers)
- Recognize (number system properties)
- Apply (estimation with whole numbers to 999, fractions, money, number system properties)
- Explain (number system properties)

Topics or Context:

- Variety of problem-solving situations using manipulatives

Skills with Targets

Notice that after each skill (verb) is a parenthetical notation. As mentioned above, I refer to these as the verb "targets." The "target" is the concept (noun or noun phrase) that the student must apply through a particular skill (verb). To just list all the verbs without these accompanying explanations would provide insufficient information. This explicitly makes the links between the "unwrapped" concepts and the "unwrapped" skills, using the same words or phrases found within the standards and indicators.

To further explain, let's look at the verb "demonstrate," the second one listed under the category of *Skills*. Referencing the original text of the first two indicators, "demonstrate" refers to "number sense, three-digit whole numbers, and simple fractions." Even though it may seem redundant to write the concepts twice (first under the concepts and again parenthetically after the skills), my reason for doing so is twofold.

First, there needs to be a clear distinction between *what* students must know and what they *must be able to do* with what they know. Students need to know what number sense *means* and then be able to *demonstrate* that understanding. Secondly, certain verbs are frequently repeated in a given standard and its related indicators. Rather than list the same verb again and again (see how "demonstrates" and "applies" are both cited more than once), and then write the concept parenthetically after each listing, it is simpler to list the verb once and parenthetically list all the different concepts that link to it, as in "Demonstrate (number sense, simple fractions, 3-digit whole numbers)."

There is an even more practical reason for listing parenthetically the concepts after the verbs. After "unwrapping," the educator should be able to put the complete text of the standard(s) and indicators aside with confidence that the graphic organizer is self-explanatory and that it represents all the concepts and the application of those concepts (the skills) needed to plan instruction and assessment.

Topics or Context

The phrase "variety of problem-solving activities using manipulatives" is fairly general. Here is where individual second-grade math teachers can decide for themselves the specific lessons, activities, text chapters, and other instructional materials they wish to use to teach their students the "unwrapped" concepts and skills. They can then list those personal choices under the heading "Topics or Context."

SECOND EXAMPLE
Grade 5 Science Standard
Scientific Inquiry

Standard: **As they increase their knowledge of <u>scientific phenomena</u>, students DEVELOP skill in using the <u>basic processes of scientific inquiry</u> by OBSERVING, DESCRIBING, ORDERING, INFERRING, COMPARING, MEASURING, CLASSIFYING, PREDICTING, FORMULATING questions, and USING data to JUSTIFY conclusions.**

Indicator: Students USE the <u>scientific method</u> to ASK and ANSWER questions about the world, including:

- ASKing questions in a form that can be investigated
- PLANning and CONDUCTing an <u>investigation</u>
- LOCATing and INTERPRETing information by using their <u>senses</u>, <u>measuring tools</u>, and <u>instruments</u> to GENERATE results in repeated investigations
- SELECT and USE a range of <u>appropriate tools</u> to QUANTIFY <u>observations of physical quantities</u>

Graphic Organizer
"Unwrapping" Scientific Inquiry Standard Grade 5

Concepts: **Need to <u>Know</u> About <u>Scientific Inquiry</u>**

Scientific Inquiry
- Scientific phenomena
- Basic investigative processes
- Conclusions
- Scientific method (how scientific inquiry gets reported)
- Investigations
- Senses
- Measuring tools
- Instruments
- Appropriate tools
- Observations of physical quantities

Skills: **Be Able to <u>Do</u>**

- Develop (Investigative Process Skills)
  - Observing
  - Describing
  - Ordering
  - Inferring
  - Comparing
  - Measuring
  - Classifying
  - Predicting
  - Formulating (questions)
  - Using (data to justify conclusions)
- Use (scientific method)
- Ask and Answer (investigative questions)
- Plan and Conduct (investigation)
- Locate and Interpret (information using senses)
- Generate (results)
- Select and Use (appropriate tools)
- Quantify (observations of physical quantities)

Topics or Context:

- Real-world investigations

This standard and its related indicator emphasize skills more than concepts. Unlike the "unwrapped" math standard in the first example, major headings in this standard and indicator are not evident. A science educator from the California Department of Education suggested grouping all the "-ing" skills in the standard under the major heading "investigative process skills." For the remaining skills listed in the indicator, I chose to capitalize the root form of the "-ing" verbs for greater emphasis. I thought the root form provided me with a more pointed reminder than did the "-ing" form that students need to be able to demonstrate each of those skills. The same could be done for the "investigative process skills," if so desired.

Notice that I included the parenthetical references only after the skills near the end of the list. When I first "unwrapped" this standard and indicator, I felt I needed those explanations there, whereas the "investigative process skills" were more self-explanatory. There is no hard-and-fast rule about when to list the parenthetical reference and when not to do so. Now I always include them to remind myself what students must be able to do with each "unwrapped" concept.

As in the second-grade math example, the topic or context of "real-world investigations" for teaching the "unwrapped" scientific inquiry concepts and skills is very general. Science educators will know their own instructional materials well enough to determine specific lessons, activities, and materials they intend to utilize.

THIRD EXAMPLE
Grade 6 History/Social Science Standards
World History and Geography — Ancient Civilizations

Standard: Students ANALYZE the geographic, political, economic, religious, and social structures of the early civilizations of Mesopotamia, Egypt, and Kush, in terms of:

Indicators:
1. the location and description (LOCATE and DESCRIBE) of the river systems, and physical settings that supported permanent settlement and early civilizations

2. the development of agricultural techniques that permitted the production of economic surplus, and the emergence of cities as centers of culture and power

3. the relationship between religion and the social and political order in Mesopotamia and Egypt (COMPARE AND CONTRAST)

4. the significance of Hammurabi's Code (Laws)

5. Egyptian art and architecture

6. the location and description of the role of Egyptian trade in the eastern Mediterranean and Nile river valley

7. the significance of the lives of Queen Hatshepsut and Ramses the Great (Influential rulers)

8. the location of the Kush civilization and its political, commercial, and cultural relations with Egypt

9. the evolution of language and its written forms

Graphic Organizer
"Unwrapping" Ancient Civilizations Standard Grade 6

Concepts: ***Need to <u>Know</u> About <u>Ancient Civilizations</u> (Egypt, Mesopotamia, Kush)***

Geographical Structures
- River systems for survival and trade
- Physical settings for permanent settlement
- Early civilizations (descriptions and locations)

Religious and Political Structures
- Relation of religion to social and political order
- Laws and influential rulers (Hammurabi's Code, Hatshepsut, Ramses)

Economic Structures
- Development of agricultural techniques
- Trade—location and description of its role in region
- Economic surplus

Social and Cultural Structures
- Cities as centers of culture and power
- Egyptian art and architecture
- Evolution of spoken and written language

Skills: ***Be Able to <u>Do</u>***
- Analyze (different structures)
- Locate and describe (river systems, physical settings, Egyptian trade, Kush civilization and its relations with Egypt)
- Compare and contrast (relationship between religion, social, political order)

Topics or Context:
- Units of study on ancient Egypt, Mesopotamia, Kush

As I contemplated how to create the graphic organizer for this "unwrapped" standard, I looked at the generally worded standard statement and realized there were no evident major headings. So I read the standard again: "Students analyze the geographic, political, economic, religious, and social structures of the early civilizations . . . ." I wondered if I could use each of those *structures* as a major heading and then simply list under each one the concepts that related to it. I did this, and it worked!

I placed my "unwrapped" version of the standard next to the original standard itself and noticed how much more user-friendly my "unwrapped" version was now that I had carefully read the standard and its indicators and represented all the concepts and skills on my graphic organizer. How much easier this would make lesson planning!

As a former sixth-grade world history teacher, I was particularly interested in this standard, as it was one I had taught my students for years. I recalled the frustration

I used to feel as I pondered how I was ever going to "cover" all the history concepts I was responsible for teaching. I realized how much the "unwrapping" process would have helped me zero in on the essential concepts and skills contained not only within this particular history standard but in all the others as well.

I also realized how any world history teacher could organize instruction of the standards around these structures and how these same structures would apply not only to ancient Egypt, Mesopotamia, and Kush, *but to every other civilization taught.* This meant less worry about "covering" all the specifics in all the assigned ancient civilizations standards sixth-graders need to learn, and more in-depth focus on the *underlying structures and related concepts* that would hold constant in every civilization.

FOURTH EXAMPLE
End of Grades 8–10
Writing Applications Benchmarks

The previous examples have focused on only one "unwrapped" standard and its related indicators. This example shows how several related *benchmarks* can be collectively "unwrapped." Benchmarks are broad statements that describe what students need to know and be able to do by the end of a particular grade span. These particular benchmarks describe what students need to know and be able to do with regard to *Writing Applications* by the end of grades 8 through 10.

A. **COMPOSE narratives that ESTABLISH a specific setting, plot, and a consistent point of view, and DEVELOP characters by using sensory details and concrete language.**

B. **WRITE responses to literature that EXTEND beyond the summary and SUPPORT references to the text, other works, other authors, or to personal knowledge.**

C. **PRODUCE letters (e.g., business, letters to the editor, job applications) that FOLLOW the conventional style appropriate to the text, INCLUDE appropriate details and EXCLUDE extraneous details and inconsistencies.**

D. **USE documented textual evidence to JUSTIFY interpretations of literature or to SUPPORT a research topic.**

E. **WRITE a persuasive piece that STATEs a clear position, INCLUDEs relevant information and OFFERs compelling evidence in the form of facts and details.**

Graphic Organizer
"Unwrapping" Writing Applications Benchmarks
End of Grades 8–10

Content: ***Need to <u>Know</u> About <u>Writing Applications</u>***

Narratives
- Setting
- Plot
- Point of view

Characters
- Sensory details
- Concrete language

Responses to Literature
- Summary
- References to:
  - Text
  - Other works and authors
  - Personal knowledge

Letters
- Business
- Letters to editor
- Job applications
- Conventional style
- Details:
  - Appropriate
  - Extraneous
  - Inconsistencies

Documented Textual Evidence
- Interpretations of literature
- Research topic

Persuasive Piece
- Clear position
- Relevant info
- Compelling evidence:
  - Facts
  - Details

(continued)

Graphic Organizer — "Unwrapping" Writing Applications Benchmarks

End of Grades 8–10 *(continued)*

Skills: ***Be Able to <u>Do</u>***

- Compose (narratives)
- Establish (setting, plot, point of view)
- Develop (characters—sensory details, concrete language)
- Write (responses to literature, persuasive piece)
- Extend (beyond summary)
- Support (references, research topic)
- Produce (letters, job apps)
- Follow (conventional style)
- Include (appropriate details, relevant info)
- Exclude (extraneous details, inconsistencies)
- Use (text evidence)
- Justify (interpretations of literature)
- State (clear position)
- Offer (compelling evidence—facts and details)

Topics or Context:

- Activities or lessons that emphasize fiction and nonfiction text forms, appropriate vocabulary, and writing for specific purposes and audiences

Since my graphic organizer is longer than the original five benchmarks, it may seem that I have complicated rather than simplified the benchmarks by "unwrapping" them. One of the things that struck me as I "unwrapped" these five benchmarks was how much information they contain. Five sentences only, but note how many concepts and skills emerge from those five sentences when they are "unwrapped." Because the concepts and skills flow so well together, I did not realize how much substance these benchmarks contained until I "unwrapped" and represented them all on the graphic organizer.

Occasionally, educators will call me over to their tables during seminar activities and say, "Our standards and indicators are written in simple enough sentences. Aren't they already 'unwrapped'?"

I share with them the above example to illustrate how deceptive such short or simplified standards and indicators may be. There is more information in standards—and benchmarks—than first meets the eye. "Unwrapping" standards, even simply worded ones, will reveal this.

Notice that I took the liberty of changing nouns into verbs (concepts into skills) in a few instances because of the way these particular indicators were worded. For example, "the <u>best summary or paraphrase</u>" seemed to naturally represent two skills students need to be able to do, namely the ability to SUMMARIZE and to PARAPHRASE. That is why they are listed in CAPS parenthetically after the underlined *concepts* of "summary or paraphrase." Students need to know the concepts of "summary" and "paraphrase." Then they need to be able to demonstrate them as *skills*.

A Guided Practice

At the end of this chapter, I have provided a Reader's Assignment to enable readers to select one or more standards and indicators of their own choosing and to practice "unwrapping" them. However, before doing this, consider trying your hand at "unwrapping" the above reading standard and its nine indicators. Because the major headings are not readily self-evident, this standard requires the "unwrapper" to work a bit harder in order to identify them from the text. Using the template on the next pages, practice "unwrapping" this standard and its indicators (a master copy of the template is included in Appendix A). When you're finished, compare and contrast how your "unwrapping" compares with my version that follows.

"Unwrapping" Content Standard

Grade Level and Content Area _____

Standard(s) and Indicators (Listed by Number Only):

Concepts: Need to <u>Know</u> About _____

*Skills: Be Able to **Do*** _____

Topics or Context: (What you will use to teach concepts and skills—particular unit, lessons, activities)

Graphic Organizer
"Unwrapping" Reading Standard Grade 12

Concepts:

Need to __Know__ About __Literary Elements__

Structural Elements of Literature
- Plot
- Theme
- Character
- Mood
- Setting
- Point of view

Understanding of Language
- Unfamiliar words (uncommon or low-frequency)
- Implied main idea
- Probable outcomes
- Details (supporting, nonsupporting)
- Summary and paraphrase

Literary Devices
- Metaphor
- Foreshadowing
- Flashback
- Allusion
- Satire
- Irony

Skills:

Be Able to __Do__

- Demonstrate (integrated understanding of language and literature; comprehension of main idea, supporting details)
- Respond (to all listed concepts)
- Predict (probable outcome)
- Summarize
- Paraphrase
- Ask and answer (questions to demonstrate comprehension)
- Compare and contrast (characters, objects, events)

Topics or Context:

- Works of fiction, specifically _____

How did you do? Did you identify similar *major headings* for the standard and related indicators? Did you identify the same or similar *concepts and skills* that you then placed under the related headings?

I selected "Structural Elements of Literature" and "Literary Devices" as two of my headings since each of them had several related concepts listed parenthetically after the heading. The third one, "Understanding of Language," I thought would serve as a good heading for the remaining key concepts.

Under the Topics or Context, I have indicated only the use of "Works of Fiction" and then left a space to determine which novels or other literary works I will later select to help students learn the "unwrapped" concepts and skills of this standard and its related indicators.

No One Way to "Unwrap"

Often I hear the question, "But what if I 'unwrap' a standard one way and a department or grade-level colleague 'unwraps' the same standard in a different way?"

There is no one right way to "unwrap" standards in terms of organization and format. The only important criterion for colleagues to remember when "unwrapping" the same standard(s) and indicators is to *make sure that the same key concepts and skills appear on each educator's graphic organizer.*

Passing the Litmus Test

After completing your graphic organizer, refer back to the original standard(s) and indicators to make certain that every key concept and skill is represented on it. In my seminars, I often say, "Here is the litmus test to determine if you have done this process correctly. Could you put away the original standard(s) and its indicators and confidently plan instruction and assessment *using only your graphic organizer,* knowing that you have faithfully captured every important concept and skill students need to learn? Would other educators identify the *same* concepts and skills?"

If the answer to both of these questions is yes, congratulations! You have successfully "unwrapped"!

A Note About Bloom's *Taxonomy*

Educators often comment that many of the skills contained within the standards and indicators can be sequenced according to the hierarchy of thinking skills. Although the skills included in te above illustrations appear in the same order as they do in the standards and indicators, taking one additional step to organize your list of skills according to Bloom's *Taxonomy* (1956) is an excellent idea. Should you choose to do so, a summary of Bloom's *Taxonomy* is included for your reference in Appendix B.

A middle school science educator called me over to his table during a seminar activity session.

"I just made a disturbing discovery as I finished circling the verbs in the standards I'm 'unwrapping.' There is only *one* skill contained in this entire standard and its indicators — *know!* I want my students to do more than just 'know' the content."

"So what will you do about this?" I asked.

"I'm going to add the other thinking skills to my graphic organizer that I also need to teach my students so they will be able to demonstrate more than simple recall of these concepts."

This conversation initiated a productive discussion with the entire group of educators. We concluded that if a particular standard and its indicators do not contain all the concepts and skills individual educators think are important and relevant to that particular standard, additions should be made to the graphic organizer with an asterisk and accompanying explanation to note the inclusion. In this way, other educators can understand why additional concepts and skills that appear on the graphic organizer do not appear in the standards themselves.

"Unwrapping" Several Standards for an Instructional Unit

Once educators become familiar with the "unwrapping" process, it is a logical next step to think about identifying all the related standards and indicators one would target in an instructional unit. For example, in a particular unit on life science or geometry, classroom educators often want to find *all* of the standards and indicators related to those particular topics, and collectively "unwrap" them.

These standards may not always be listed together in the standards documents, however. Often they appear in several places within grade-level or course-specific standards and require "sleuthing" to find them all. Educators do this because they want to take a more holistic approach in their instructional planning, not just teaching the standards in bits and pieces as they randomly appear in the standards documents or in the textbook, but grouping related ones together for more effective instruction and greater student understanding.

Once all of the associated standards and indicators are identified for a particular unit or set of lessons, educators then collectively "unwrap" them, create their graphic organizer, and plan instruction and assessment to address all the concepts and skills contained in those related standards.

Power Standards

In my companion volume, *Power Standards* (2003), I present a proven process for prioritizing the standards to identify the ones that "matter the most" for student success. Power Standards are a subset of the complete list of standards and indicators for each grade and for each subject. They represent the "safety net" of standards each teacher needs to make sure that every student learns prior to leaving the current grade. Students who acquire this "safety net" of knowledge and skills will thus exit one grade better prepared for the next grade.

When considering which standards and indicators are "power," think of the ones that students need for success according to the following three criteria: (1) what they need to know and be able to do in school this year, next year, and so on; (2) what they need to learn in the way of life skills; and (3) what they need to know and be able to do on all high-stakes district and state assessments.

Make distinctions between which standards are "essential" and which ones are "nice to know." Teach the "essentials" for depth of student understanding. Then teach the "nice to know" standards as they relate to the ones identified as "essential."

There is a great need for such a two-tier distinction since all standards and indicators are *not* of equal importance. Because there is simply not enough time to thoroughly teach and assess every standard and indicator, it is critical for educators to decide which standards are absolutely essential for student success and then allocate instructional time accordingly.

Star the Power Standards Concepts and Skills

The logical next step for educators who have already identified their Power Standards is to "unwrap" them! When "unwrapping" Power Standards, educators want to know what to do about other related standards and indicators that have not been so designated but are taught along with the Power Standards in a particular unit.

If they directly relate to the Power Standards you are targeting, "unwrap" them also, and when you create your graphic organizer, star or bold or highlight the concepts and skills derived from the Power Standards. In this way, you will be alerted as to which concepts and skills you need to emphasize the most with students, especially if they represent state-tested concepts and skills.

"Unwrapping" Tested Standards

A related question is this: "What if district or state assessment results indicate that students are scoring low on a particular standard or indicator that has *not* been designated a Power Standard?"

Whether or not it is a Power Standard makes no difference. If, according to the test results, students need more in-depth understanding of the concepts and skills within a particular standard or indicator, then what better way for teachers to really zero in on where students are having trouble than by "unwrapping" that tested standard or indicator? They can then plan instruction and assessment to help students become proficient in those critical concepts and skills. Students will then be better able to demonstrate that proficiency on district and state assessments.

Standards, Not Standardization

The process of "unwrapping" is a powerful technique for managing standards effectively. In seeking to familiarize educators with this process, the goal is not *standardization* of teaching styles and techniques; the goal is to *effectively teach students the standards*. Educators may collectively "unwrap" the same standard and indicators in the same way, but they must always be encouraged to draw upon their own individual talents, creativity, experience, and expertise in helping their students gain a deep understanding of the concepts and skills within the standards they have "unwrapped."

Getting Everyone Involved

Once educators learn this process and have sufficient opportunity to practice it, they may wish to begin sharing "unwrapped" standards and indicators with their grade-level or department colleagues. Even if the format of their colleagues' graphic organizer differs from their own, as long as all necessary concepts and skills are represented there, educators can confidently use another's graphic organizer to plan their own instruction and assessment. In this way, every educator does not have to personally "unwrap" every standard that he or she must teach.

Chapter Four describes how educators are "working smarter, not harder" by dividing up all the standards and indicators in different content areas and collaboratively "unwrapping" them. They are then sharing their "unwrapped" standards, Big Ideas, and Essential Questions with one another. This saves educators time, results in more focused instruction, and leads to a corresponding increase in student learning.

Next Step: The Big Ideas

Once your targeted standards are "unwrapped," what's the next step? It is to help students realize why these concepts and skills are important for them to learn. In the next chapter, you will learn how to derive Big Ideas from the "unwrapped" standards and why doing so is one of the most powerful instructional strategies educators can use to help students retain what they have been taught long after instruction ends.

Reader's Assignment

Time for independent practice! Choose a particular content area and grade. Open your standards and find one or more standards and related indicators you would like to "unwrap." Classroom teachers may wish to select standards they will be targeting in an upcoming unit of instruction.

"Unwrap" your selections by underlining the concepts (nouns) and circling the skills (verbs). Then create a graphic organizer in a format of your choosing to represent all of your "unwrapped" concepts and skills. After reading the next chapter, you will have the opportunity to review your "unwrapped" standards and indicators and then determine the Big Ideas you want students to derive from their study of those same concepts and skills.

CHAPTER TWO

Finding the Big Ideas

Why Big Ideas?

Do you remember any particularly challenging high school or college exams on which, despite their difficulty, you scored quite well? If you were to take those same tests now, do you think you could do as well today as you did then?

I know that I could not. The reason? Much of what I learned in high school and college I simply memorized for a specific test. Once the test was over, so was my retention of that particular information. I had no larger framework or structure of understanding in which to place the voluminous number of facts I was striving to remember, nor did I see much relevance of the information to the whole of my life. Because I have never again needed much of that information, it has remained "out of sight, out of mind."

In his article entitled, "The Standards Juggernaut," educational consultant Marion Brady (2000) states: "Give adults the exams they took a few years earlier in high school or college, and their poor performance will prove that facts that are not made part of an often-used, larger scheme of meaning are soon forgotten."

Mr. Brady goes on to say what many educators are realizing: Students need "large-scale mental organizers" or "big ideas" to help them organize and make sense of the myriad facts they are expected to learn. The lessons from brain research have acknowledged the fact that the human brain organizes information according to patterns. Unless educators deliberately help their students connect the concepts and skills being taught to prior learning through some type of organizational structure, Mr. Brady concludes that "facts will continue to come first" with little chance that "some master pattern will eventually emerge to bind (the facts) together in a way that makes useful sense."

Educators need to help students connect the dots of understanding. In order for students to discover these larger concepts *on their own,* they need learning opportunities that allow them to "wrestle with ideas and understand them at a deep level" (Merrill Area Public Schools, Merrill, Wisconsin, 1999). These "key principles and generalizations [are] . . . the 'big ideas' that transfer through time and across cultures" (Erickson, 2000).

Grant Wiggins and Jay McTighe refer to Big Ideas as "enduring understandings" and define them as "the important understandings that we want students to 'get inside of' and retain after they've forgotten many of the details" (1998).

The Deep End of the Pool

I call Big Ideas the "deep end of the pool." For the majority of educators I have worked with, identifying Big Ideas does not come easily at first. Why? Because most will confide that they themselves were not taught to think in terms of Big Ideas during their own educational experience. Yet their recognition of the importance of doing this, along with a corresponding willingness to find out how, are rooted in a strong desire to help convey to their students what they *know* is important for students to learn on their own.

Fortunately or unfortunately, it is not enough simply to say to students, "Here's the Big Idea you need to know," and then proceed to tell them what that Big Idea is. If it were this easy, we could simply tell students how everything relates to everything else and be done with the challenge of helping them make these discoveries on their own. We would never again see students engage in the struggle to make their own connections between present and past learning—*the critical factor in the learning process that begins with **not** knowing.*

As the saying goes, "If teaching were merely 'telling,' we would all be so smart we wouldn't know what to do with ourselves!" We all know that what lasts is what we conclude on our own.

What *Are* Big Ideas, Anyway?

What exactly *are* Big Ideas and how do we help students realize them? Big Ideas are what Oprah Winfrey calls "lightbulb moments," those sudden flashes of illumination when a student says, "Oh, I get it!" and goes on to articulate the meaning s/he has suddenly derived.

Here are several statements that attempt to define what Big Ideas are. I am listing them in bulleted form and isolating each one from the others so that you can reflect on each one's meaning more effectively and choose the one or more that best define the concept for you.

- Big Ideas are those "Aha!" realizations, discoveries, or conclusions that students reach *on their own* either during or after instruction.

- Big Ideas are key generalizations students can articulate after their sudden grasp of the "big picture."

- Big Ideas are the lasting understandings students will take with them on their forward educational journey.

- Big Ideas are personally worded statements derived from a deep understanding of the concepts under investigation.

- Big Ideas are open-ended, enduring ideas that transfer understanding from one subject to other areas of study.

A working definition of Big Ideas will be helpful for the explanations, illustrations, and practice activities that follow in this chapter, but the reasons why the Big Ideas are so powerful and why they endure long after instruction ends are even more important—*students discover the Big Ideas for themselves and articulate those ideas in their own words.*

A Powerful Illustration

Big Ideas lie at the very heart of an area of study. They bring into focus the unifying characteristics of a broad topic, theme, or discipline. They represent in-depth understanding of the "unwrapped" concepts under investigation versus tedious memorization of those concepts as isolated facts merely to be recalled.

I am indebted to Connie DeCapite, Director of FIRST (Fullerton International Resources for Students and Teachers) at California State University, Fullerton, California, for sharing with me the following conversation she overheard from two students on campus. I continue to relate this story all over the country because it *shows* how learning endures long after instruction ends when educators deliberately organize instruction to help students discover the Big Ideas.

The two young men had just emerged from a history class holding their returned papers from a rigorous essay exam. They stopped in the corridor to read the professor's remarks and see the points awarded.

"Oh, man, I blew that test!" said one of them. "I couldn't remember anything about that particular revolution in Asia!"

"So what did you write?" asked the other.

"Nothing! My mind just went blank! I got a zero!"

"I couldn't remember a thing about it either," said the other. "But as I sat there trying to come up with *something* to write, I remembered that in high school one of my history teachers had said to us in class one day, 'How many of you know that all revolutions throughout history have certain attributes in common?'

"This was news to all of us, so he went on to say, 'Tell you what. I'll teach you what those attributes are, and then you can find out for yourself if I'm right or not.'

"After teaching us the common attributes, he had us examine several revolutions in different eras of history to see if we could identify those attributes in each and every one of them. And it was true! The same ones appeared in every revolution regardless of the era in which it took place!"

The first student asked, "So what did you write on the exam?"

His classmate immediately flipped through the pages of his test booklet to the problematic essay question and read his first sentence aloud as if he were a celebrated expert on the subject.

"'*As in all revolutions, there are certain common, underlying attributes.*' And then I just went on to describe each of those general attributes without ever addressing the specifics of the one asked for on the test."

"So? How did you do?" the first student asked.

"Better than I thought. Listen to this."

He turned the essay booklet sideways to read aloud the professor's remarks written in the margin next to the awarded 15 points.

"*Nice job summarizing the attributes of revolutions <u>in general</u>. However, you were supposed to discuss the attributes of this revolution <u>in particular</u>!*"

Because that student had been fortunate enough to have had a teacher help him discover the Big Idea about revolutions in high school, he was able, years later, to successfully transfer that same knowledge to a new and unfamiliar situation.

Guidelines to Determine Big Ideas

Here are a few guidelines adapted from different sources to assist you in determining your own Big Ideas from the standards and indicators you "unwrap."

- Will this Big Idea apply to more than one content area of learning?

- Will this Big Idea apply to more than one grade in school?

- Will this Big Idea endure? Will it be as important in the future as it is now?

- Will this Big Idea be one that students remember long after instruction ends?

Attributes of Big Ideas

Joan Benton and Chalyn Newman of the California International Studies Project, based at Stanford University in Palo Alto, California, have identified four attributes of Big Ideas based on their work with the Program for Complex Instruction and Dr. Rachel Lotan:

- *Brevity*—usually five to ten words

- *Conceptual*—cannot be answered factually or with a yes/no statement; goes beyond content to conjecture

- *Open-ended*—allows for multiple perspectives; no one "right" answer

- *Enduring*—a "timeless" idea that may apply to other fields of learning.

More Than Just One Sentence

The Big Idea statement represents the kernel of understanding we want students to comprehend independently and remember indefinitely. The beauty of the Big Idea statement is its brevity. However, students certainly should be expected to expound on that succinct statement if asked to do so, just as they are taught to write a topic sentence and then elaborate upon that main idea with supporting detail sentences. Otherwise, the Big Idea may be reduced to a factual statement response to the Essential Question. In the next chapter, I will share a powerful teaching strategy that every educator can use every day to help students develop their ability to identify and elaborate on the Big Idea.

How the Graphic Organizer Helps Identify Big Ideas

Most educators agree that it is much easier to identify Big Ideas after the standards and indicators have been "unwrapped" and represented on a graphic organizer, rather than trying to determine them from the original standards text.

One of the reasons I like to create headings on the graphic organizer is that it makes the identification of Big Ideas much easier than trying to determine them by looking at a comprehensive bulleted list without such headings. Certainly there are instances when an educator can take one look at a bulleted list of concepts and quickly identify the Big Ideas. Experienced educators are often so familiar with the content they teach that they already know or can easily determine the inherent Big Ideas. But when the Big

Ideas are not self-evident, grouping the concepts under headings and then looking at one section at a time is an easy way to start. Just identify one Big Idea for each section. This is not to say there must always be a one-to-one correspondence of Big Ideas with major headings; often two Big Ideas can be derived from one section. The Big Ideas should *collectively reflect the most important student understandings for the entire list of "unwrapped" concepts and skills.*

Educators have repeatedly said to me that they like using the graphic organizer to identify their Big Ideas because it gives them a practical way of moving from the "concrete" (the actual concepts and skills that students need to learn and be able to do) to the "abstract" (the enduring understandings or generalizations they want students to derive from the particular standard).

Let us now revisit the examples of "unwrapped" standards and indicators from the last chapter, beginning with grade 2 mathematics and ending with grade 12 reading, to see how Big Ideas can be derived from the identified concepts and skills found within them. All five graphic organizers from Chapter One are reprinted here in Chapter Two for easier reference.

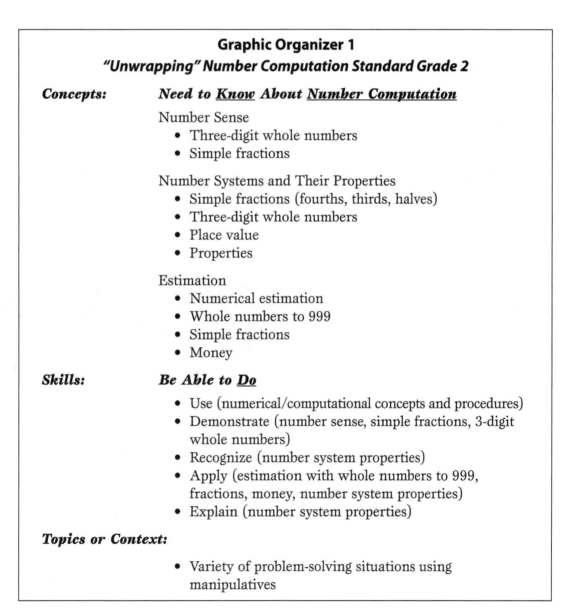

Graphic Organizer 1
"Unwrapping" Number Computation Standard Grade 2

Concepts: ***Need to <u>Know</u> About <u>Number Computation</u>***

Number Sense
- Three-digit whole numbers
- Simple fractions

Number Systems and Their Properties
- Simple fractions (fourths, thirds, halves)
- Three-digit whole numbers
- Place value
- Properties

Estimation
- Numerical estimation
- Whole numbers to 999
- Simple fractions
- Money

Skills: ***Be Able to <u>Do</u>***

- Use (numerical/computational concepts and procedures)
- Demonstrate (number sense, simple fractions, 3-digit whole numbers)
- Recognize (number system properties)
- Apply (estimation with whole numbers to 999, fractions, money, number system properties)
- Explain (number system properties)

Topics or Context:

- Variety of problem-solving situations using manipulatives

Number Computation Big Ideas from "Unwrapped" Standard and Indicators

1. Numbers can represent different quantities or amounts.

2. Fractions represent quantities less than, equal to, or greater than one whole.

3. The position of a digit determines its value in a number.

4. Estimation comes close to an actual number.

Derive Big Ideas from Concepts or Skills?

Notice that because this "unwrapped" standard emphasizes number sense, number system properties, and estimation, the Big Ideas must reflect the foundational understandings that students need in this regard. Students need to first *know* these concepts and then be able to "use, demonstrate, recognize, apply, and explain" them.

Usually educators determine the Big Ideas from the *concepts* more than they do from the skills, because the concepts represent the essential understandings we want the students to take away from a standards-based unit or course of study. This is not to minimize the importance of the skills, however. It is often in the *exercise of those related skills* that students arrive at the "aha" understandings about the concepts. Thus, concepts and skills together lead to students' realization of the Big Ideas.

Jane's Quiet Wisdom

It may be stating the obvious, but I think it is important for educators to think deeply during instructional planning about what it is they want students to learn as a result of instruction. I always remember the quiet wisdom of Jane Cimolino, my mentor teacher with 35 years of classroom teaching experience, who first introduced me to the concept of Big Ideas.

As we planned an integrated history/social science and language arts unit for our middle school students, Jane said to me, "The study of history should never be reduced to having students memorize a mountain of facts they will rarely ever retain. So I always try to think of the three or four Big Ideas I want the students to be able to explain to me in their own words after instruction ends. I then strive to help them connect these Big Ideas to their own lives. If I don't, history has no real meaning for them."

Big Ideas represent that deep thinking, the end result we want students to "walk away with" and see as relevant to their own lives. It is the educators who first decide the Big Ideas in order to be clear about their instructional goals. But it is the students who ultimately will *say* them. That is why educators often word their Big Ideas in *student-friendly language.*

Student-Worded Big Ideas

Wouldn't second-grade teachers be thrilled if, after instruction targeted at the above "unwrapped" math standard and indicators, the following question-answer exchange took place between themselves and their students?

Teacher: "So what have you learned about numbers in the unit we have just completed?

Students: "Where a digit is in a big number shows what it's worth!"

Teacher: "Excellent! That's one of the important Big Ideas I was hoping you would learn!"

Adults often exchange intellectual ideas using language that is beyond the understanding of most students. Because educators are master communicators, they know inherently how to express complex ideas in an understandable way to their students, whatever age their students may be. That is why, after articulating the Big Ideas in language they themselves might use, a powerful next step in the Big Idea identification process is for educators to think how to write those Big Ideas in student-friendly wording.

I regularly meet educators who tell me, "I usually think in terms of how students say things anyway, so I just naturally wrote my Big Ideas in words my students would most likely use." If you are one of these educators, great! If not, the next paragraph may assist you in doing this.

After you have drafted your Big Ideas, ask yourself, "How would the students say these?" Think in terms of making the Big Ideas *conversational*. The easiest way to do this is to look at an adult-worded Big Idea, extract the essence of that statement, and then substitute simpler language.

From Adult-Worded to Student-Worded Big Ideas

The following examples of Big Ideas, which I identified from a Midwestern state's writing standards, show how to "translate" adult-worded Big Ideas into student-worded versions.

1. Narratives (fictional writings) need a specific setting and supporting details to advance plot.

   Stories need a place to happen with details that keep readers interested.

2. Descriptive (nonfiction) writing develops a main idea with supporting details.

   The strongest nonfiction writing explains an idea completely.

3. Different types of writing communicate information for a variety of purposes and audiences.

   Writers need to know how to communicate in different ways for different people.

One of my favorite student-worded Big Ideas came to my attention with a burst of laughter from a group of upper elementary educators in Stockton, California. They knew they had hit "pay dirt" with this one, created by Gary Colburn of Harrison School.

"The first time you write something is not the last!"

Gary explained that his students always resist the rewriting of *any* written work. He knew that if he could somehow help his students realize that Big Idea on their own, he would never again have to continually cajole and persuade them to revise their writing.

A Double-Lens Search for Big Ideas

In searching for the inherent Big Ideas contained within an "unwrapped" standard, I try to see it from both the educator's and the students' points of view. I endeavor to capture both the educator's end learning goals *and* the students' purpose for learning.

I look at the graphic organizer and ask myself the following questions.

"Okay, so what? If I teach my students these concepts and skills, what do *I* want them to realize at a deeper level of understanding than mere recall of information?"

Because I'm so accustomed to thinking from the perspective of "what's in it for the students?" I then try to identify what I hope *students* will deeply understand about the concepts and skills related to the "unwrapped" standard. How will they express these Big Ideas in their own words? Hopefully, my resulting Big Ideas will satisfy both of these points of view.

Topical Big Ideas

There are *topical* Big Ideas that relate primarily to the inherent understandings in a particular course of study or section of the standards. An example of a *topical* Big Idea for algebra would be: "Polynomials can be simplified by addition, subtraction, multiplication, and division," an important topical learning outcome for Algebra I students to realize.

All four of the grade 2 math Big Ideas listed above are topical Big Ideas. They are limited to number sense in mathematics. There is nothing wrong with this, especially when one is first beginning the practice of identifying Big Ideas. Also, topical Big Ideas stand alone on their own merit, because they represent the foundational understandings or "building blocks" we want to be sure students achieve relative to a particular area of study.

Broader Big Ideas

But there are also *broader* Big Ideas, the generalizations derived from one area of study that connect to and can be found in several subject matter areas. Once educators become accustomed to identifying topical Big Ideas, they can take a broader view and ask, "What connections can I make between these Big Ideas to those that extend beyond one content area only?" In this way, educators can see the interrelationship between *topical* Big Ideas so as to formulate *broader* Big Ideas. By expanding their own understanding in this way, they will be better able to teach their students how to eventually make such generalizations on their own.

Let's look again at the graphic organizer for grade five science and the Big Ideas that were gleaned from the "unwrapped" concepts and skills, two or three of which typify *broader* Big Ideas.

Graphic Organizer 2
"Unwrapping" Scientific Inquiry Standard Grade 5

Concepts: **Need to <u>Know</u> About <u>Scientific Inquiry</u>**

Scientific Inquiry
- Scientific phenomena
- Basic investigative processes
- Conclusions
- Scientific method (how scientific inquiry gets reported)
- Investigations
- Senses
- Measuring tools
- Instruments
- Appropriate tools
- Observations of physical quantities

Skills: ***Be Able to <u>Do</u>***

- Develop (investigative process skills)
  - Observing
  - Describing
  - Ordering
  - Inferring
  - Comparing
  - Measuring
  - Classifying
  - Predicting
  - Formulating (questions)
  - Using (data to justify conclusions)
- Use (scientific method)
- Ask and Answer (investigative questions)
- Plan and Conduct (investigation)
- Locate and Interpret (information using senses)
- Generate (results)
- Select and Use (appropriate tools)
- Quantify (observations of physical quantities)

Topics or Context:

- Real-world investigations

Scientific Inquiry Big Ideas from "Unwrapped" Standard and Indicators

1. Scientific inquiry is a systematic process for understanding the natural world.

2. Investigative process skills combined with specific tools help us ask and answer questions about how life works.

3. Knowledge gained from one investigation helps us make sense of new and different situations and challenges.

4. People can justify their conclusions with observable data.

As I stated in the last chapter, when I first "unwrapped" this standard, I regarded it as more skill-based than concept-based. Notice that the first Big Idea is the only one that is clearly derived from the *concept* of scientific inquiry. The remaining three Big Ideas represent conclusions that we hope students would reach after applying the "unwrapped" *skills*.

Also, the first Big Idea is a definition of scientific inquiry and certainly more *topical* in nature than the remaining three, which are *broader* Big Ideas. To illustrate this idea, I often ask educators to look again at number four, "People can justify their conclusions with observable data," and then I pose the following questions:

> "This Big Idea is based in the content area of science. But couldn't it also be applicable to mathematics? How about to language arts, if students are writing a persuasive essay and need to support their main ideas with details and factual data?"

Educators often ask students these same kinds of questions to help them begin looking beyond the topical Big Ideas for the connections between one discipline and another.

If you are particularly knowledgeable in the content area of science, do you "see" different Big Ideas in the "unwrapped" concepts and skills represented on the graphic organizer from those presented above? Also, my four Big Ideas are adult-worded. How might the students articulate them? As practice, try wording them as students might.

Not a "Cookie Cutter" Process

As you review any of the above Big Ideas or those that are to follow, you may derive different Big Ideas from the "unwrapped" standard(s) and indicators than the ones I have written. Or you may find a more precise way to express the same ones. Writing Big Ideas can be challenging, tricky, and even frustrating at first. There is no "cookie cutter" approach to doing so. I always encourage educators to first brainstorm Big Ideas and then go back and revise them until they are happy with the results, just as they encourage students to revise their first drafts of an important piece of writing. As with almost every challenging new task, the more one does it, the easier it gets. The mind starts to think in terms of Big Ideas and becomes increasingly articulate in identifying them.

Seminar participants always say at the end of the day that it was a very helpful practice to look at first-draft Big Ideas created and shared by other seminar participants and then immediately review their own first drafts. This practice helps educators revise Big Ideas that may be too broad or too narrow and recognize ones that are "just right." It helps them identify the ones that are topical, see the ones that are broader in nature, and rework those that need just a bit more "tweaking."

This collaborative learning process results in a quality enhancement of everyone's Big Ideas. It's always fun to see which Big Ideas shared by seminar participants get the "ooh" or "ahh" response from the audience—that intuitive recognition that the Big Idea has expressed an essential truth or captured the essence of an important realization.

Let us now revisit the graphic organizer of our third example of "unwrapped" standards and indicators to see how the Big Ideas were derived from the middle school history/ social science standard and indicators.

Graphic Organizer
"Unwrapping" Ancient Civilizations Standard Grade 6

Concepts: **Need to _Know_ About _Ancient Civilizations_ (Egypt, Mesopotamia, Kush)**

Geographical Structures
- River systems for survival and trade
- Physical settings for permanent settlement
- Early civilizations (descriptions and locations)

Religious and Political Structures
- Relation of religion to social and political order
- Laws and influential rulers (Hammurabi's Code, Hatshepsut, Ramses)

Economic Structures
- Development of agricultural techniques
- Trade—location and description of its role in region
- Economic surplus

Social and Cultural Structures
- Cities as centers of culture and power
- Egyptian art and architecture
- Evolution of spoken and written language

Skills: **Be Able to _Do_**

- Analyze (different structures)
- Locate and describe (river systems, physical settings, Egyptian trade, Kush civilization and its relations with Egypt)
- Compare and contrast (relationship between religion, social, political order)

Topics or Context:

- Units of study on ancient Egypt, Mesopotamia, Kush

Big Ideas from the Standard's Introduction

In this particular standard, I received additional insights for deciding my Big Ideas from an unexpected source—the *Introduction* section of the standards relating to Ancient Civilizations. This *Introduction* not only provided an overview of the standards to follow but also conveyed the "big picture" understandings or Big Ideas students need to understand as a result of study. For this reason, I encourage educators to refer to the *Introduction* sections included throughout the state standards as valuable guides for formulating their Big Ideas.

Note the phrases I underlined in this **Introduction to Ancient Civilizations** and see how these influenced my own Big Idea identification below.

World History and Geography
Ancient Civilizations

Introduction

Students in grade six expand their understanding of history by studying the people and events that ushered in the dawn of the major western and nonwestern ancient civilizations. <u>Geography is of special significance</u> in the development of the human story. Continued emphasis is placed on the <u>everyday lives, problems, and accomplishments of people,</u> <u>their role in developing social, economic, and political structures</u>, as well as in <u>establishing and spreading ideas</u> that helped transform the world forever.

Students develop higher levels of critical thinking by considering <u>why civilizations developed where and when they did, why they became dominant, and why they declined.</u>

Students analyze the <u>interactions among the various cultures</u>, emphasizing their <u>enduring contributions</u> and the <u>link, despite time, between the contemporary and ancient worlds</u>.

Ancient Civilization Big Ideas from "Unwrapped" Standard, Indicators, and Introduction

1. Geography affects the way societies function.

2. Civilizations require geographic, political, economic, religious, and social
   structures in order to survive and thrive.

3. Each structure plays a unique and interconnected role with other structures for the survival of the civilization.

4. The effects of human actions combined with environmental factors determine whether a civilization ceases to exist or continues to survive.

5. Contemporary civilizations parallel those of the past.

How Many Big Ideas?

Because this particular standard is one that my mentor, Jane Cimolino, and I had taught together for years, we had already identified Big Ideas similar to the ones above. Jane used to caution me about having too many Big Ideas, however.

"If we want the students to really understand ancient civilizations, then we need to focus on only three or four Big Ideas for a particular unit. Otherwise we are not going to achieve the depth we need to reach for students to understand and remember the information that is most important."

I have exceeded Jane's recommended number of Big Ideas by one in the above list of five Big Ideas. But I felt that each one was a key understanding for students to gain. Also, I knew that each of these would extend beyond the boundaries of any single civilization and have relevancy *across* civilizations, both ancient and modern, as students continued their study of history in subsequent years of schooling.

Jane believed that three or four Big Ideas are about right for a unit of instruction lasting several weeks. Joan Benton and Chalyn Newman of the California International Studies Project recommend having only *one* Big Idea or broad generalization that is critical for students to grasp by the culmination of a unit of study. Again, there is no set rule as to how many Big Ideas an educator should identify. This is a matter of professional choice. I recommend identifying only as many Big Ideas as are needed to collectively represent the "unwrapped" concepts and skills students need to learn.

My Big Ideas in Students' Words

The Big Ideas above may not yet be student-friendly enough for middle school students, and three of the five certainly exceed the ideal length of five to ten words. But I remember my students' responses to the following wrap-up discussion question I posed to them at the conclusion of our Ancient Egypt and Mesopotamia unit. I thought their versions expressed more succinctly and accurately the essential understandings I wanted them to have than did my adult-worded ones.

"So what do you think were the most important things you learned during this particular unit?"

One student exclaimed, "Wow, I didn't realize that every civilization on earth has the same structures!"

Another added, "Or that the structures all work together to keep the civilization going!'

Or this last one that proved Jane's assertion that students must be able to see the connection between what we teach them and their own lives: "Our society today is a lot like those that aren't around any longer."

What teacher of this content area wouldn't be thrilled for students to grasp and articulate these insights? When I heard my own students expressing their own meaning from what I had tried so hard to help them realize, I experienced anew the joy that comes to every teacher when his or her students "light up" with new understandings.

Helping students grasp the Big Ideas calls to mind a nugget of Far Eastern wisdom about teaching that I read over a quarter of a century ago: True education is not a "pumping in" of information, but a "drawing out" from the learner the understanding already present within.

Let us look again at our fourth example of "unwrapping" and see how Big Ideas can be identified from the concepts and skills listed on the graphic organizer. Remember that in this illustration five benchmarks (learning outcomes to be achieved by the end of a grade span) were collectively "unwrapped."

Graphic Organizer
"Unwrapping" Writing Applications Benchmarks
End of Grades 8–10

Content: ***Need to <u>Know</u> About <u>Writing Applications</u>***

Narratives
- Setting
- Plot
- Point of view

Characters
- Sensory details
- Concrete language

Responses to Literature
- Summary
- References to:
  - Text
  - Other works and authors
  - Personal knowledge

Letters
- Business
- Letters to editor
- Job applications
- Conventional style
- Details:
  - Appropriate
  - Extraneous
  - Inconsistencies

Documented Textual Evidence
- Interpretations of literature
- Research topic

Persuasive Piece
- Clear position
- Relevant info
- Compelling evidence:
  - Facts
  - Details

(continued)

Skills: ***Be Able to <u>Do</u>***

- Compose (narratives)
- Establish (setting, plot, point of view)
- Develop (characters—sensory details, concrete language)
- Write (responses to literature, persuasive piece)
- Extend (beyond summary)
- Support (references, research topic)
- Produce (letters, job apps)
- Follow (conventional style)
- Include (appropriate details, relevant info)
- Exclude (extraneous details, inconsistencies)
- Use (text evidence)
- Justify (interpretations of literature)
- State (clear position)
- Offer (compelling evidence—facts and details)

Topics or Context:

- Activities or lessons that emphasize fiction and nonfiction text forms, appropriate vocabulary, and writing for specific purposes and audiences

Visiting the *Introduction* Again

As I pondered what the Big Ideas might be for these "unwrapped" benchmarks, I decided again to consult the *Introduction* section for clues. Note in the following *Introduction to Writing Applications* what this particular state has determined are important understandings for students to achieve. I have again underlined those phrases that reflect this. Note the similarities in my resulting Big Ideas.

Introduction: Writing Applications

End of Grades 8–10

Students need to understand that <u>various types of writing require different language, formatting, and special vocabulary</u>. Writing serves <u>many purposes</u> across the curriculum and takes <u>various forms</u>. <u>Beginning writers learn about the various purposes of writing</u>; they attempt and use a small range of familiar forms (e.g., letters). <u>Developing writers are able to select text forms to suit purpose and audience</u>. They can explain why some text forms are more suited to a purpose than others and begin to use <u>content-specific vocabulary</u> to achieve their communication goals. <u>Proficient writers control effectively the language and structural features of a large repertoire of text forms</u>. They deliberately choose <u>vocabulary to enhance text</u> and structure their writing according to <u>audience and purpose</u>.

Writing Application Big Ideas from "Unwrapped" Writing Benchmarks and Introduction

1. Fiction and nonfiction forms of writing each have their own unique formats, vocabulary, language, and style.

2. Proficient writers choose different forms of writing to meet their specific purpose for particular audiences.

3. The most effective fiction and nonfiction writing supports its major points with relevant facts and details.

Even though this *Introduction* describes the characteristics of both beginning and developing writers, I decided to focus my Big Ideas on what it has to say about *proficient* writers. The graphic organizer notes the specific concepts and skills students need to know and be able to do by the end of the grade eight through ten writing program, but the *Introduction* identifies the Big Ideas that the student-demonstrated proficiency of these specifics should ultimately yield. The specific concepts and skills will provide the learning vehicles for students to reach the destination of the Big Ideas.

Here again is the fifth and final example, an "unwrapped" grade 12 reading standard and its related indicators and the Big Ideas I developed while reviewing the graphic organizer.

Graphic Organizer
"Unwrapping" Reading Standard Grade 12

Concepts: ***Need to <u>Know</u> About <u>Literary Elements</u>***

Structural Elements of Literature
- Plot
- Theme
- Character
- Mood
- Setting
- Point of view

Understanding of Language
- Unfamiliar words (uncommon or low-frequency)
- Implied main idea
- Probable outcomes
- Details (supporting, nonsupporting)
- Summary and paraphrase

Literary Devices
- Metaphor
- Foreshadowing
- Flashback
- Allusion
- Satire
- Irony

Skills: ***Be Able to <u>Do</u>***

- Demonstrate (integrated understanding of language and literature; comprehension of main idea, supporting details)
- Respond (to all listed concepts)
- Predict (probable outcome)
- Summarize
- Paraphrase
- Ask and answer (questions to demonstrate comprehension)
- Compare and contrast (characters, objects, events)

Topics or Context:

- Works of fiction, specifically _____

This example provided me with an easy way to identify Big Ideas from the original text of the standard and its indicators when they are not readily apparent. I simply determined one Big Idea for each of my three concept headings by asking:

- "What is the Big Idea for *structural elements of literature*?"
- "What is the Big Idea for *understanding of language*?"
- "What is the Big Idea for *literary devices*?"

My answers to these questions became the following Big Ideas.

Literary Elements' Big Ideas from "Unwrapped" Standards and Indicators

1. Every work of fiction utilizes the same series of literary elements.

2. Comprehension of fiction is dependent upon the ability to apply techniques of skilled readers.

3. Literary devices enhance and deepen fiction's impact upon the reader.

Big Ideas Often Contain a Benefit

One of the personal insights I have gained as I continually present this material to educators is that often the Big Idea statement contains within it a *benefit* for learning a particular concept or skill. Look again at the third Big Idea above. The benefit of learning literary devices is contained in the phrase "enhance and deepen fiction's impact upon the reader."

To identify such a benefit when writing Big Ideas is especially important considering the number of times students moan, "Why do we have to learn this?" or "When will we ever use this in real life?"

Instead of an educator trying to "tell" students why literary devices are important, wouldn't it be marvelous if students, upon completion of a novel that was rich in literary devices, could announce to the teacher, "Now I understand why you made us learn metaphors, allusion, satire, and irony! The novel we just read was so much more interesting because you taught us those literary devices, then asked us to identify them in the novel, and tell why they were important to the story. They really got me into the imaginary world of the author. Now I understand *why* this is a great book!"

The students, on their own, have identified the Big Idea, stated it in their own words, and discovered the benefit for learning it! The likelihood is high that they will retain this understanding long after this particular instructional focus is over.

Should We Post the Big Ideas in the Classroom?

From time to time I hear the question from educators, "If the Big Ideas are so important, why not post them on the classroom wall? Then we can simply announce to students, 'This is what I want you to learn in this course or unit.'"

Even though it is a powerful practice for an educator to think about and identify the Big Ideas for a particular unit of study prior to instruction, simply announcing the Big Ideas to students at the inception of a unit may eliminate their motivation to discover those desired end results of learning for themselves. From the students' point of view, this may sound as if the teacher is saying, "I have already realized these Big Ideas, and now you get to have that same experience." Remember that the power of Big Ideas lies in the practice of expecting students to *discover them on their own.*

To promote student interest and engagement, consider withholding the Big Ideas from the students and instead posting open-ended *Essential Questions* on the classroom walls at the beginning of an instructional unit. Then announce to students that they will explore these questions in depth during the course of the unit and that by its end, they will be able to answer these questions with Big Ideas stated in their own words.

In the next chapter we will explore the third and final component of the "unwrapping" standards process—Essential Questions—and the vital role they play in focusing both instruction and assessment.

Reader's Assignment

Refer again to the graphic organizer you created for the standard(s) and indicators that you selected to "unwrap" at the conclusion of the last chapter. Ask yourself, "What are the Big Ideas I want the students to discover on their own after learning these concepts and skills?"

Keep this simple. Brainstorm two, three, or four Big Ideas without worrying about the exact wording. You can revise them later. Once you have your Big Ideas in reasonably good shape, see if you can "translate" them into student-friendly language.

Your Big Ideas will be your road map and your guide as you plan and deliver instruction. At the conclusion of the next chapter, you will write Essential Questions, review your Big Ideas, and see if those Big Ideas indeed answer your Essential Questions!

CHAPTER THREE

Writing the Essential Questions

Which engages student attention more, questions or facts?

Consider this *fact:* "Fractions represent quantities less than, equal to, or greater than one whole." This is indeed a mathematical Big Idea that we certainly want students to know, but merely *telling* them this fact may spark little resulting interest. It is a discovery that has already been made—by someone else. It is static or flat in terms of *motivating* students to get actively engaged in the activities needed to grasp this understanding firsthand.

The following pair of related questions, on the other hand, presents a challenge to learners.

"What is a fraction? What is its relationship to a whole number?"

These two questions invite students into the learning process. They advertise upfront the learning expectations. They provide the catalyst that will eventually lead students to understand for themselves what their teachers want them to learn. Educators refer to these two questions as they plan the learning experiences students will need in order to reach the important conclusion that fractions do indeed "represent quantities less than, equal to, or greater than one whole."

Consider how the following questions derived from different content areas would stimulate student interest to find out the answers:

- Are our resources renewable?

- Why do people create art?

- Are rights equal for everyone? What makes you think so?

- Are all of the pioneers really gone?

- What makes something alive? Are there any nonliving things that have life characteristics?

- Is there a solution to every problem? How do you know?

- Why should you be physically active?

- As a speaker, why do you need to know your audience?

- Why write your own music?

- Why is teamwork a necessary life skill?

Questions such as these may *appear* quite simplistic because of their plain and concise wording. Yet the learning that results through students' pursuit of the answers to these questions, through active engagement in carefully selected lessons and activities, will be anything but simplistic.

I especially like the following Essential Question, by Gary Colburn of Harrison School, Stockton USD in Stockton, California, to lead his students to their own discovery of the Big Idea about the value of the writing process.

"Why can't I write something only once?"

Wouldn't it be great if students could answer this question for themselves, and in their own words, as follows: *"Writing is rewriting! I can't get it exactly the way I want it the first time!"*

Imagine the gratitude of every educator in later grades who no longer had to motivate students to work through the steps of the writing process because those students had already realized the need for doing so in a prior grade!

Standards-Based Essential Questions

Questions deliberately selected to drive instruction and assessment for a particular unit of study are known by many names, a few of which include Guiding Questions, Focus Questions, Enduring Questions, Essential Questions, etc. I have chosen the term "Essential Questions" because I see the role of these questions as exactly that in terms of advancing student understanding: *essential*.

The Essential Questions are no ordinary questions. Because they are derived from the "unwrapped" standards and indicators, they are, in truth, *standards-based questions*. This is an important distinction, as every state now recognizes its own academic content standards as the comprehensive list of learning outcomes its students are to learn. Thus, educators can represent the essential concepts and skills embedded in the wording of the standards as thoughtfully determined Essential Questions and then use these questions to drive both instruction and assessment.

Big Ideas: The Answers to the Essential Questions

When educators pose the Essential Questions to students at the inception of an instructional unit, they are advertising upfront the learning goals they expect students to meet. They then use the Essential Questions and "unwrapped" concepts and skills as instructional filters for selecting lessons and activities that will advance student understanding toward those learning goals. As students move through the lessons and activities, they are developing their understanding of the "unwrapped" concepts and skills and formulating their responses to the Essential Questions.

Remember that the ultimate goal in this regard is for students to be able to *answer the Essential Questions with the Big Ideas expressed in their own words*.

Providing Evidence That Students Meet the Standards

The oral and written responses students give through formal and informal assessments aligned to the Essential Questions provide the evidence as to whether or not the students have met the particular standard(s) and indicator(s) upon which they are based.

To what *degree* students demonstrate proficiency can be determined with the help of a particular rubric or scoring guide designed to evaluate their responses.

Topical or Broad Essential Questions

Just as Big Ideas may be either *topical* (reflecting specific learning outcomes for a particular unit or focus of study) or *broad* (reflecting learning applicable to other areas *beyond* a particular unit or focus of study), Essential Questions may also be designated as either topical or broad. As you review the examples of Essential Questions later in this chapter and in the grade-span chapters to follow, it may be helpful to identify whether you think the Essential Questions are topical or broad. This will assist you in the writing of your *own* Essential Questions.

The Power of Questioning Techniques

Educators have long known the power of using questioning techniques to engage students and evoke insightful responses from them. In his article, "What Is a Good Guiding Question?" (1998), Rob Traver of the Massachusetts Department of Education offers these characteristics of guiding (essential) questions:

1. Open-ended, yet focus inquiry into a specific topic

2. Nonjudgmental, but answering them requires high-level cognitive work

3. Contain "emotive force" and "intellectual bite," such as "Whose America is it?" and "When are laws fair?"

4. Succinct—"a handful of words that demand a lot."

Questions that cannot be answered with a simple "yes" or "no" or with the mere recall of facts indeed demand more of students. These questions can set the purpose for learning that requires students to think, make connections, draw conclusions, and justify their responses with supporting details. Effective questioning techniques lie at the heart of a thinking curriculum.

Dr. Douglas Reeves frequently asserts, "We need great teachers doing what they do best—encouraging students to think, reason, write, and communicate their understanding." Essential Questions promote such exemplary practices.

Higher-Level Questions

In my high school journalism class, I remember learning that every nonfiction article should convey certain key information in the first paragraphs. This information is referred to as "the five W's"—who, what, where, when, why—and how. However, not all of the "W's" convey equally important information. The first four in the above list usually represent lower-level thinking skills that require only recall of facts. It is the "why" and "how" questions that will always move the level of thinking to a higher level, because the "why" and "how" questions require the learner to *apply* the information in any number of ways.

This is not to undermine the value of students acquiring a knowledge base through the judicious use of "who, what, where, and when" questions posed by the instructor. The problem is that too often learning can stop here if educators do not deliberately ask higher-level questions. When this is the case, students accumulate a body of facts but are not shown how to extend their knowledge into the interpretative, evaluative, and synthetic levels. It is in these higher levels that students integrate the new information they are studying with their own prior knowledge, make connections to other areas of study, and learn how to reason, infer, and draw insightful conclusions.

Reflecting on my own 24 years of classroom teaching experience, I believe that the very best questions expect students to effectively respond to *both* lower- and higher- level types of questioning. I call these types of combination questions "one-two punch" questions.

"One-Two Punch" Essential Questions

The "one-two punch" is a two-part question. The first part asks students to demonstrate their *recall* of information. It validates the need to acquire a knowledge base. The second part asks them to *apply* that information. It communicates the message that facts alone are not enough; they must be utilized if they are to be of real value.

Here are a few examples of "one-two punch" Essential Questions from different content areas:

- What is the writing process? Why do accomplished writers use it?

- What is the difference between oil and acrylic paints? How does an artist decide which medium to use?

- What are linear equations? How can we use them in real life?

- What does "working out" mean? How does it help you?

- What is musical notation? How does it help a performer sing or a musician play a particular instrument?

- What are the elements of an effective computer presentation? Why is visual design important to such a presentation?

Let us now look at the Essential Questions for each of the five examples of "unwrapped" standards and indicators, beginning with grade 2 mathematics and ending with grade 12 reading. The Essential Questions are answered in parentheses by the corresponding Big Ideas reprinted from Chapter Two. Note how any "one-two punch" questions ask students for specific knowledge and then challenge them to go beyond mere recall.

Note also how certain Big Ideas as *written* may only be a definition or factual statement, or seem to answer only one part of a two-part Essential Question. Remember, the initial goal when writing a Big Idea is to capture in one sentence the most important idea students need to grasp about the particular content they are studying. As you review the following Essential Questions with their corresponding Big Ideas, decide if an additional Big Idea is needed. I have indicated in the accompanying commentary where you might wish to expand on the Big Idea responses.

Lastly, let me reiterate that identifying Big Ideas cannot be reduced to a "cookie cutter" process. There is always room for improvement, and this naturally occurs with continued practice. The same holds true for the wording of Essential Questions. You may think of an even more profound Big Idea or Essential Question for the examples below than the ones provided.

> **Essential Questions Answered by Big Ideas Example 1**
> *Grade 2 Number Computation*
>
> 1. **What are numbers? How do we use them?**
>   (Numbers can represent different quantities or amounts.)
>
> 2. **What is a fraction? What is its relationship to a whole number?**
>   (Fractions represent quantities less than, equal to, or greater than one whole.)
>
> 3. **Why isn't a digit always worth the same amount?**
>   (The position of a digit determines its value in a number.)
>
> 4. **What is estimation? When and how do we use it?**
>   (Estimation comes close to an actual number.)

Are the "one-two punch" questions in number one above both answered by the Big Idea? Do you think an additional Big Idea statement is needed that more directly addresses the second part of the question? How about in number two? One could argue that the Big Idea as stated does indeed meet the demands of both questions. Now look at number three. This Big Idea conveys the essential understanding regarding place value. However, in the two-part question of number four, the Big Idea statement only provides a definition of estimation. An additional Big Idea such as "Estimation is used when an exact answer is not needed" would satisfy the second question.

There is usually a direct, one-to-one correspondence between Big Ideas and Essential Questions, but this is not an imperative. Educators may see the need to identify two Big Idea statements in response to one Essential Question or to a "one-two punch" Essential Question.

> **Essential Questions Answered by Big Ideas Example 2**
> *Grade 5 Scientific Inquiry*
>
> 1. **What is scientific inquiry? How and when can it be used to understand and explain scientific phenomena?**
>   (Scientific inquiry is a systematic process for understanding the natural world.)
>
> 2. **What are the skills and knowledge needed to conduct a scientific inquiry? How does scientific inquiry help us learn about the way life works?**
>   (Investigative process skills combined with specific tools help us ask and answer questions about how life works.)
>
> 3. **How can we apply what we've already learned to new and different situations?**
>   (Knowledge gained from one investigation helps us make sense of new and different situations and challenges.)
>
> 4. **Why gather data?**
>   (People can justify their conclusions with observable data.)

The Big Idea in number one above only defines scientific inquiry. What additional Big Idea could be added to address the second part of the question? In the second and third Essential Questions, both Big Idea responses are key understandings for students to achieve, but both of them are a bit too long. How might students say each of these in fewer words?

I like both the Essential Question and its corresponding Big Idea in number four because of their versatility. The Essential Question is simple, concise, and open-ended. It can be asked of students in both elementary and secondary grades. Both the Essential Question and the Big Idea response can apply not only to science but to other content areas as well, such as mathematics and language arts, particularly the writing of a persuasive paragraph or essay (as explained in Chapter Two). In addition, both the Essential Question and the Big Idea response can be defined as either *topical* or *broad*.

Essential Questions Answered by Big Ideas Example 3
Grade 6 History/Social Science

1. **What role did geography play in the ancient civilizations of Egypt, Mesopotamia, and Kush? What role does it play in modern civilizations?**
   (Geography affects the way societies function.)

2. **Why do civilizations develop certain organizational structures?**
   (Civilizations require geographic, political, economic, religious, and social structures in order to survive and thrive.)

3. **How do these structures impact each other?**
   (Each structure plays a unique and interconnected role with other structures for the survival of the civilization.)

4. **Why do certain civilizations no longer exist?**
   (The effects of human actions combined with environmental factors determine whether a civilization ceases to exist or continues to survive.)

5. **What links can be made between the cultures, structures, and contributions of the ancient world to contemporary societies?**
   (Contemporary civilizations parallel those of the past.)

The first part of the two-part Essential Question in number one above is open-ended, but it is decidedly *topical*. It specifically addresses the role geography played in these ancient civilizations. The second part of the two-part question is *broader;* it asks students to make connections to present-day civilizations. Even though both questions begin with "What," they demand more than mere recall of facts. The Big Idea response is *broad* because it applies to both ancient and modern times. It is an essential understanding that students can grasp from their study of people and places in elementary grades and later build upon in the secondary grades when they learn about other civilizations, both ancient and contemporary.

In the second Big Idea, a more succinct, student-friendly version might be "Every civilization needs certain structures to survive." What might students say in their own words for the Big Ideas in number three and four? To help students articulate the Big Ideas in student-friendly terms, ask them to think about what they might say in a real conversation with a younger student or what they would say to their parents to summarize what they had learned in a particular unit of study. In this way, a student-worded Big Idea response to the Essential Question in number four might be, "How humans live and interact with nature determines whether we live or die."

Essential Questions Answered by Big Ideas Example 4
End of Grades 8–10 Writing Applications

1. **What distinguishes different forms of fiction and nonfiction writing?**
   (Fiction and nonfiction forms of writing each have their own unique formats, vocabulary, language, and style.)

2. **Why do writers choose a particular form of writing to express their ideas?**
   (Proficient writers choose different forms of writing to meet their specific purpose for particular audiences.)

3. **How do writers strengthen the points they are trying to convey to their readers?**
   (The most effective fiction and nonfiction writing supports its major points with relevant facts and details.)

These three Essential Questions and their corresponding Big Ideas accurately reflect the benchmarks (grade-span learning objectives) from which they were derived, and the Big Ideas do answer the Essential Questions. Whether students at the conclusion of grade 10 would use the same wording to describe their understandings is open for discussion, but they certainly could.

Essential Questions Answered by Big Ideas Example 5
Grade 12 Reading

1. **How is fiction organized to tell a story effectively?**
   (Every work of fiction utilizes the same series of literary elements.)

2. **Why are knowledge of comprehension techniques and the ability to apply them important to readers in today's world?**
   (Comprehension of fiction is dependent upon the ability to apply techniques of skilled readers.)

3. **What are literary devices? Why do authors use them?**
   (Literary devices enhance and deepen fiction's impact upon the reader.)

In responding to the first Essential Question above, students need to know what the literary elements (setting, character, plot, resolution, etc.) actually *are* before they can realize that every literary work contains them. Replacing the original question with a "one-two punch" question as follows might better ensure this: "What are the structural elements of literature? How are all literary works alike?" Knowing what those elements are, especially for grade 12 students, may be an implied expectation of *prior* learning, but the Big Idea and Essential Question(s) are reflective of this particular standard and its indicators.

The second Essential Question establishes a purpose for learning. It asks students to determine for themselves *why* they should learn the various comprehension techniques. The Big Idea provides that answer.

The first time I wrote my third Essential Question, it looked like this: "How do literary devices enhance and deepen the fictional reading experience?" I didn't realize then that I had merely rephrased my Big Idea as a question! In so doing, I had already provided the answer I wanted *students* to realize. There was no further learning required. Now it is a "one-two punch" question that demands more of students; they must demonstrate recall of knowledge (definitions of specific literary devices), and they must determine authors' purpose for using those devices (to enhance and deepen the fictional reading experience).

Which to Write First — Big Ideas or Essential Questions?

I recommend to educators that they first identify the Big Ideas and then craft engaging Essential Questions that will establish the purpose for learning. To use a metaphor for this relationship, think of the Big Ideas as the "desired travel destination." By identifying the Big Ideas first, educators decide the final destination of the learning journey for students. The "advertised" Essential Questions will hopefully get the "travelers" excited about making the "trip," and the lessons and activities selected by the educator will provide the "vehicle" to enable students to get there.

Frequently, seminar participants will comment, "It was much easier for me to write the Essential Questions than it was to come up with the Big Ideas." This may be because writing an open-ended question to elicit the already identified answer is simply easier to do. The deepest thinking has already taken place in the determination of the Big Idea. Once the Big Idea is decided, it is fun to think of a provocative lead-in question.

The truth is, it does not matter which of the two you determine first. Honor your own process. What *is* important is to maintain the question-answer relationship between your Big Ideas and your Essential Questions.

A Powerful Use of Essential Questions

The following narrative account illustrates the most effective classroom use of Essential Questions I have yet encountered, a powerful practice that every educator in every grade and every content area can use.

The story tells of a secondary mathematics educator who uses the Essential Questions to advance student understanding toward her advertised "learning destinations" *in each and every lesson.* Whenever I share this story in my seminars, I preface it with the promise, "This will be worth the price of admission!" I include it here in hopes that you will consider using the Essential Questions in the same way.

A few years ago, Sue Sims, a high school mathematics teacher in Vista Unified School District, Vista, California, invited me to visit her geometry class to show me how she was implementing in her instructional program the ideas from my first book co-authored with Jan Christinson, *Student Generated Rubrics* (1998). On the morning of my visit, there were only a few minutes of class time remaining, so I sat down at the back of the room to wait.

Looking around, I noticed mathematical questions written in colorful, large letters on narrow butcher paper and posted all around the perimeter of the classroom near the ceiling. These questions asked:

- What is the Pythagorean theorem? When and how is it used?

- What is the perimeter of a geometric shape, and how is it found?

- What is the area of a geometric shape? How do you calculate the area of triangles, rectangles, parallelograms, and trapezoids?

- What is a linear equation? What are two methods that can be used to graph a linear equation?

My attention was brought back to Ms. Sims as she asked the students to put away their books and materials and give her their undivided attention.

She then announced, "Now I want all of you to look again at our Focus Questions for this geometry unit posted around the room. Think about what we just finished doing in class. Which question did we work on today? What new insights and understanding have you gained?

Several students raised their hands to respond.

In my later years as a classroom educator, I had discovered the value of posting the Essential Questions on the wall so students would know what I expected them to know and be able to do on my end-of-unit assessment, but I had not gone the extra step of using the questions in such a powerful way. Ms. Sims had recognized the importance of helping her students identify and connect the new information and skills they had gained in that particular lesson with her ultimate learning goals. Her Focus Questions were clearly guiding her instruction, and she was reminding her geometry students—daily—that these questions represented what she expected them to know by the conclusion of the unit.

After her students departed, I expressed my enthusiasm for the self-reflection opportunity she had provided her students.

Sue replied, "I really have to discipline myself to stop teaching, assign homework, and ask students to do this exercise with me, especially because we are on such a tight bell schedule. But it occurred to me that if I really want the students to achieve my learning goals for them, then I have to help them make those connections every single day."

It will be no surprise to readers that Ms. Sims' end-of-unit geometry assessment exactly matched her advertised learning goals—the posted Focus Questions. She shared with me several samples of proficient and exemplary student work from prior unit assessments that she had also matched to the Focus Questions for those units. The students' work provided highly persuasive evidence that her powerful practice of regularly helping students make the connections between the Focus Questions, daily lessons, and summative assessment was definitely a practice worth emulating.

Sue concluded, "When this unit is over, I will put up my Focus Questions for the next unit. This has done so much to improve the performance of my students!"

I predicted to Sue that her powerful practice would ultimately benefit other educators and students, and so it has! Educators from around the country who have heard this story are reporting similar results after utilizing the Essential Questions in the same way.

Taking This Practice One Step Further

Recently, a pre-service teacher in one of my seminars listened to this story and said, "This has gotten me thinking. Since writing is so important for student understanding, I think I will ask students to make these important connections by writing one or two sentences in their journal at the end of each lesson about what they just learned relative to the Essential Questions. This will give them a written record of their understanding as it develops throughout the unit."

One veteran teacher in the room looked over at this brand new educator and said, "What a great idea! I wish I'd thought of that myself! I'm going to use that!"

Whether we ask students to process their own learning verbally or in writing, the *regular, consistent practice* of asking them to connect each day's lesson to the Essential Questions is what will keep students moving successfully along the highway to the end destination of the Big Ideas.

Extended Response Writing Assessment

Because students know at the beginning of an instructional unit that they will be expected to answer the Essential Questions at the conclusion of a unit, educators often utilize the Essential Questions as their summative assessment. They simply ask students to head a piece of notebook paper and then write their full responses to the Essential Questions. Students write each Big Idea in their own words as a topic sentence and then support it with further explanation and details. This is a wonderful way to differentiate assessment because it allows every student to demonstrate as much as s/he has individually learned relative to the Essential Questions. Also, since the Big Ideas have been derived from the "unwrapped" concepts and skills, student responses will almost certainly include the understanding and application of the specific "unwrapped" concepts and skills that students have learned during daily instruction and related activities.

When students are assessed in this way, they are often amazed to realize how much they have learned as they write responses that reflect "all that they know" about each Essential Question. If a rubric or scoring guide has been developed for this type of extended response assessment, the work produced by the students not only provides the evidence that the standards have been met but also the degree of proficiency the students have attained.

Curt Greeley and Chris Grisaffi, two experienced history teachers at Righetti High School in Santa Maria, California, use the Essential Questions as their essay questions on unit exams rather than the essay questions provided in the textbook.

They explain, "The Essential Questions are directly based on the standards we 'unwrap' and the concepts and skills we identify from those standards. If students can answer the Essential Questions, their responses will give us more valuable feedback about what they have truly learned relative to the standards than we can derive from their responses to textbook essay questions."

Curt shared with me that since he started "unwrapping" his history standards and using Essential Questions to help students realize the Big Ideas, he has noticed a marked improvement in the level of student learning as compared to the days before he used this process.

Wonderful testimony, indeed!

"Working Smarter, Not Harder"

Educators appreciate the practicality and usefulness of the "unwrapping" standards process, but often they express concern regarding the additional planning time this will require. In Chapter Four, I will share how educators are finding ways to "work smarter, not harder" as they set out to collaboratively "unwrap" K-12 standards in targeted content areas.

Reader's Assignment

Now it's your turn! Try writing Essential Questions that will lead students to their own discovery of your Big Ideas. After you complete your first draft of Essential Questions, ask yourself:

- Are my Essential Questions open-ended?

- Will they be engaging for students?

- Will they take students beyond the "who, what, where, and when" recall of information to the "how" and "why" applications and extensions of learning?

- Do my Big Ideas succinctly and effectively answer my Essential Questions?

CHAPTER FOUR

Getting Everyone Involved in the Process

Everyone in education today is working harder than ever before. Each of us has more work to do than can be done within the hours available. The implementation of new practices and programs to meet the increasing demands placed on educators and administrators alike is contributing to what Dr. Douglas Reeves refers to as "initiative fatigue." To prevent the "unwrapping" process from adding to this fatigue rather than alleviating it, this chapter addresses ways educators can "work smarter, not harder" with regard to "unwrapping" their standards.

Where Is the Time to Do This?

I remember one elementary educator who, in the first minutes of my seminar, announced in frustration loud enough for all to hear, "So, on top of everything else I have to do, now I have to *'unwrap' the standards!* I just don't have time to do this! Why doesn't the state just hire you to come in and 'unwrap' all of our standards *for* us?"

I looked at the rest of my audience to gauge their reaction to her outcry. Many were nodding in silent agreement.

I thought a moment and answered, "Well, first of all, no one has offered me any money to do this!"

Everyone laughed. The group relaxed. But I had more to say on the subject.

"As logical as your request is, how do you feel when you are just 'handed' a new binder of information—that you had no part in designing—and told to implement it?"

The elementary educator immediately replied, "I don't like it!"

I continued, "Isn't your personal involvement in a process more likely to ensure that you not only understand but will actually *use* the final product in your own classroom?"

"Absolutely," came the answer.

To all the participants I replied, "Then, if you will, let me take you through this 'unwrapping' process today, and when we are finished, I'll ask you for your honest opinions as to whether or not you think this will help improve your instruction and your students' learning. If your answer is 'yes,' then we'll discuss practical ways to 'work smarter, not harder.' Fair enough?"

Everyone agreed, and we got to work. By mid-afternoon, the group had worked through the entire process—including the identification of Big Ideas and Essential Questions.

There had been an almost palpable shift in the energy level of participants from when we had started that morning. The educators had become enthusiastic as they began to see the tremendous value and practicality of this process.

How to "Work Smarter, Not Harder"

The time came to discuss implementation. Without a workable plan that lightened—rather than increased—everyone's workload, I knew that many present would evaluate the seminar positively but not necessarily implement these ideas in their own instructional programs—the true mark of effective professional development.

"Okay, everyone, the moment of truth has arrived. How many of you see value in what we have done today?"

Hands went up all over the room.

"That's great! There's only one snag. What are we going to do about the question asked this morning—the one about how to find the time needed to 'unwrap' all your standards? Would you now like to discuss how to 'work smarter, rather than harder' in this regard?" I asked.

I had everyone's full attention.

"Before I do, let me ask you this. Do you think it is necessary for *every* educator to go through the experience of learning how to 'unwrap' standards *at least once*?"

"Yes!" was the audience response.

I continued, "Once an entire group of educators learns how to 'unwrap' and recognizes firsthand the value of doing so, individuals get together by grade level in elementary and by departments in secondary. They simply divide up the standards and indicators in a selected content area, 'unwrap' the ones they've agreed to do, and share their completed work with colleagues. Many districts are putting their "unwrapped" standards, Big Ideas, and Essential Questions on their websites so everyone in the district can access the work that's been accomplished."

The group could see how this practical way to "work smarter, rather than harder" would indeed lighten their workload instead of adding to it. I went on to give them the specifics as to *how* and *when* this happens.

How *Elementary* Educators Implement These Ideas

Once educators assemble by grade levels at the elementary level to collaboratively "unwrap," a decision must be made: Either target one particular content area or "unwrap" different content areas simultaneously. There are benefits to either approach.

Elementary educators within the same building usually want to "unwrap" all the standards and indicators in one content area, beginning with either language arts or math. The grade-level groups determine a time frame or schedule for doing this, knowing that the "unwrapping" work will proceed much more quickly the second time because everyone is already familiar with the process. In this way, each selected content area is "unwrapped," one after the other, until all the work is finished.

The second approach moves the "unwrapping" process along in *more than one* content area at the same time. Groups form according to content areas, and every educator chooses to work in a particular grade level within a specific content area group. Obviously, more time may be needed to "unwrap" several content areas simultaneously if the groups of educators are small and the number of standards and indicators in each content area is large. I recommend that there be at least two educators representing each grade level, if at all possible. The valuable discussion that occurs when two or more grade-level educators collaborate will result in a better quality of "unwrapped" products.

If the group is large, sufficient grade-level representation in each targeted content area will be easier to arrange. The large number of standards and indicators in several content areas can be distributed among the grade-level group members, and the work can be completed in less time.

When arranging district-wide meetings to "unwrap" the elementary standards, content area coordinators typically plan and facilitate the process. Each school sends grade-level and/or content area representatives who collaborate in grade-level teams to "unwrap" the standards. After the work is finished, the collections of "unwrapped" standards with accompanying Big Ideas and Essential Questions are made available to all the elementary educators within the district. But again, I must emphasize the importance of *everyone* first learning the "unwrapping" process before distributing collections of "unwrapped" standards and indicators. Personal experience with this process is a prerequisite for truly effective implementation.

How *Secondary* Educators Implement These Ideas

Secondary educators invariably organize themselves by content-area departments. Within any department, educators are naturally interested in first "unwrapping" the standards for the specific courses they teach. Once each member of the department learns the process, the task of "unwrapping" all the standards and indicators for a particular content area can be accomplished in a relatively short amount of time.

I observed a high school history department chairperson allocate the standards to be "unwrapped" within his department as follows.

He said, "Since I teach the Cold War, I'll 'unwrap' the Cold War standards and indicators. John, you do the ones for your World War II course, and Michelle, you 'unwrap' the U.S. history standards."

He continued in the same way, asking the remaining members of his department to "unwrap" the particular standards and related indicators they themselves taught. By the end of a few department meetings in which a portion of the time was allocated to "unwrapping," these educators were able to complete the work, including the identification of Big Ideas and Essential Questions.

As each secondary department independently completes the "unwrapping" of its own standards and indicators, the cumulative result will be "unwrapped" standards, Big Ideas, and Essential Questions for every curricular department in the school. These collections can then be posted on the school or district website for easy access and reference by all of its educators.

Suggested Big Ideas and Essential Questions

I advise educators who will be sharing their "unwrapping" work with colleagues to consider adding the adjective "Suggested" in front of the Big Ideas and Essential Questions they write. In this way, individual educators who perhaps identify different Big Ideas and Essential Questions than those of their colleagues can exercise their own judgment in deciding what the ideas and questions should be. When educators review the work of their colleagues, they usually do agree with the Big Ideas and Essential Questions as written, but if not, they have a starting place for determining their own.

A Range of Perspectives

Most educators, once they experience firsthand the "unwrapping" process, see great value in sitting down with colleagues to divide up the standards and indicators and "unwrap" some—but not all—of the standards they personally teach. They then enjoy discussing ways to share their "unwrapping" work, Big Ideas, and Essential Questions in order to prevent everyone from having to "reinvent the wheel."

I appreciated the honesty and candor of the elementary educator described at the beginning of this chapter who did not want to "unwrap" the standards herself, hoping instead that someone else would do the work and then just give it to her. This perspective, however, is more the exception than the rule. Every once in a while an educator expresses a viewpoint that represents the opposite end of the spectrum.

Will Sibley, history teacher at Ben Davis Junior High in Wayne Township, Indianapolis, attended my fall "unwrapping" seminar for his district's secondary educators. When the day concluded, Will expressed a wish to continue "unwrapping" the standards and indicators he personally taught in his history courses. Knowing I was to repeat the seminar the next day for the district's elementary teachers, I suggested to Will and Catherine Cragen, his teaching colleague with whom he had collaborated during the day, that they ask their principal for permission to return the next day to continue their work.

The following day, both Will and Catherine were back! I arranged for them to sit away from the large group so they could collaborate without interruption. When they departed that afternoon, they told me that having that extra day immediately following the initial seminar to continue "unwrapping" enabled them not only to get more of their standards "unwrapped," but that it really "cemented" their understanding of the entire process.

The following spring I conducted a meeting in Wayne Township for teachers from the different schools who had been asked by their principals to assist colleagues within their own buildings as "standards coaches." I was happy to see Will in attendance.

The discussion eventually turned to ways in which we might organize all the teachers in the district to collectively "unwrap" all the K-12 standards in language arts, math, science, and social studies. Will raised his hand to speak.

"I understand that it is time-consuming to 'unwrap' all our standards, and I do agree that it's a good idea to talk about ways to expedite this process district-wide," he said. "But I have to tell you, after 'unwrapping' *all* the standards and indicators I personally teach, it has completely changed my instruction. Because I am now crystal clear about what my students need to learn, I'm teaching better than ever before, and the work the students are producing is far superior to anything I've received in past years. So I just want to go on record as saying that there is great value for teachers to personally do all of their own 'unwrapping.'"

I saw the indisputable wisdom in Will's perspective, one that spoke volumes about what this practice can do for any educator willing to engage fully in the work it requires.

Once "Unwrapped," Forever "Unwrapped"

"Unwrapping" all the standards is certainly going to require an investment of time to accomplish, but the good news is this: Once a standard is "unwrapped," it is "unwrapped" forever. Certainly I do not mean *forever* in the literal sense. If and when the standards are significantly revised at the state or district level, there may indeed be changes in the standards that are substantial enough to warrant a second "unwrapping." But until then, educators and students will benefit from current efforts of educators to "unwrap" all their standards. The work completed now will greatly help educators teach their students the "unwrapped" concepts and skills and guide them to discover the Big Ideas through the standards-based Essential Questions.

But When Do Educators Do This?

When implementing any new practice, however valued, the problem is always finding sufficient time to do so when many other matters require attention. Often grade-level teams at the elementary level and department teams at the secondary level "unwrap" their grade-specific standards as the year progresses during their regularly scheduled faculty, grade-level, or department meetings.

To facilitate this at faculty meetings, administrators set the agenda so that business matters can be discussed during the first 20 minutes of an hour meeting, and the remainder of the time can then be used for "unwrapping" standards. In this way, a significant amount of "unwrapping" work can be accomplished in several meetings over the course of a year. This idea of providing educators with job-embedded collaboration time focused on practices to improve instruction and student achievement is becoming increasingly popular.

However, I wish to present another point of view regarding the time issue. If educators can be periodically released from teaching responsibilities for larger blocks of time—half days or even full days—a great deal of "unwrapping" work can be accomplished at higher levels of quality than by parceling out such work at the end of the instructional day when people are tired. I have repeatedly observed the best results in finished "unwrapped" products when educators are mentally fresh, their focus is concentrated and sustained, and they are able to collaborate for longer blocks of time without interruption.

The Spiral Effect

Consider the positive impact on students within a school district if all of its educators from kindergarten through high school made it their regular practice to "unwrap" standards, identify Big Ideas, and pose Essential Questions. With each successive year of schooling, students would be able to build upon a solid foundation of concepts and skills gained the previous year. They would become accustomed to articulating their understanding in terms of Big Ideas and in making connections between new information and what they already know. After several years, the cumulative results in terms of student learning would be dramatic indeed.

By working collaboratively to "unwrap" all the standards, educators are helping each other to utilize more quickly this effective practice in their own instructional programs, thereby moving such an idealistic vision one step closer to reality.

Reader's Assignment

Think about and discuss with colleagues how to implement a systematic plan for "unwrapping" standards, identifying Big Ideas, and writing Essential Questions for one or more content areas in a particular grade or department, in an individual school, or in the entire school district. As you plan for implementation, you may wish to refer to Chapter Nine for a summary checklist of the steps to follow in the entire "unwrapping" standards process.

CHAPTER FIVE

Primary Standards "Unwrapped"

In this chapter dedicated to the primary grades, kindergarten through grades 2 or 3, I have included numerous examples of "unwrapped" standards and indicators from several content areas, particularly language arts, mathematics, science, and social studies. You may also wish to review the upper elementary examples in the next chapter. Several of these may be adaptable to primary grades.

These "unwrapped" examples were created by me and by seminar participants in different states. I have received permission from these educators to reprint their work for the publication of this book. A few of the examples included were submitted anonymously during the guided practice "unwrapping" activity at the seminar.

Please note: I have not included the full text of the standards and indicators along with the graphic organizer of "unwrapped" concepts and skills. Although inclusion of the full text would indeed have been helpful, particularly for educators in the individual states from which the "unwrapped" standards originate, printing limitations made this infeasible. Certain examples do identify particular states and standards, however.

Lastly, a few of the graphic organizers do not include parenthetical "targets" after the skills. The educators involved either chose not to include them, or they attended one of my earlier "unwrapping" standards seminars where I did not emphasize their importance to the degree that I do now.

The central purpose for including these examples is to provide readers with a wide variety of graphic organizers, Big Ideas, and Essential Questions in several content areas that they can reference to more fully comprehend the "unwrapping" process. To all those who have generously contributed to this collection of examples, I thank you on behalf of all educators whose understanding of how to "unwrap" will deepen as a result of your work.

LANGUAGE ARTS — Reading
Kindergarten
Wayne Township[1]
Indianapolis, Indiana

Concepts: ***Need to <u>Know</u> About <u>Reading Comprehension</u> <u>Strategies</u>***

Indiana Language Arts Standard 2

Framework
- Title
- Name of author

Connections
- Life experiences
- Familiar stories

Understanding
- Main ideas
- Plot
- Picture clues
- Context clues
- Predictions
- Story

Skills: ***Be Able to <u>Do</u>***
- Locate
- Use
- Connect
- Retell
- Identify
- Summarize
- Predict

Big Ideas

1. Finding pictures and words on the cover helps you choose a good book.

2. Using story clues (picture clues, context clues, predictions) helps us understand a story.

3. Connecting stories to our life helps us understand the story.

4. Retelling a story helps us remember the story's main idea.

Essential Questions

1. Why do book companies put pictures and words on our books?

2. What do we do to understand a story?

3. How do our memories help us understand a story?

4. Why do you like to retell stories?

[1] Reprinted with permission.

LANGUAGE ARTS — Reading
Grade 2
Kristin Parisi[2]
Chapelwood Elementary
Wayne Township
Indianapolis, Indiana

Content:

Need to __Know__ About __Reading__
Standard 1: Word Recognition, Fluency, and Vocabulary Development

Phonemic Awareness
- Beginning, middle, and ending sounds
- Rhyming words
- Blends and vowels

Decoding and Word Recognition
- Spelling patterns
- Words with more than one syllable
- Abbreviation
- Plural words and irregular plurals
- Voice and expression

Vocabulary and Concept Development
- Antonyms and synonyms
- Compound words
- Prefixes and suffixes
- Multi-meaning words

Skills:

Be Able to __Do__
- Demonstrate and distinguish (beginning, middle, and ending sounds; rhyming words)
- Pronounce (blends)
- Recognize and Use (spelling patterns)
- Decode (words with more than one syllable)
- Identify and Use (regular and irregular plurals)
- Read (with voice expression)
- Understand and Explain (antonyms and synonyms)
- Use and Predict (compound words)
- Know (prefixes and suffixes)
- Identify (multi-meaning words)

Topics or Context:

- Basal reader
- Trade books
- Poetry
- Letter writing
- Narratives
- Descriptive writing

---

[2] Reprinted with permission.

(continued)

Big Ideas

1. Words have beginning, middle, and ending sounds along with vowel sounds and possibly blends.

2. Readers use knowledge about a variety of skills in order to decode and recognize words.

3. Proficient (skilled) readers learn new words by knowing about synonyms, antonyms, compound words, prefixes, suffixes, and multi-meaning words.

Essential Questions

1. Do letters make sounds and sounds make words? What makes a word?

2. How do you figure out a new word when you are reading?

3. How do you learn what new words mean?

LANGUAGE ARTS—Reading
End of K–3
Author

Concepts:

Need to <u>Know</u> About <u>Reading Process Strategies</u>
By the End of Ohio K–3 Reading Program

Purpose for reading

Literary passages

Predictions

Text clues

Conclusions

Strategies and skills
- Comprehension
- Self-monitoring

Information
- In text
- Between text
- Across subject areas

Questions
- Literal
- Informational
- Evaluative

Skills:

Be Able to <u>Do</u>
- Establish (purpose for reading)
- Use (comprehension strategies)
- Understand (literary passages, text)
- Make and support (predictions)
- Cite (examples)
- Draw (conclusions)
- Apply and adjust (skills, strategies, self-monitoring)
- Summarize (info)
- Compare and contrast (info)
- Demonstrate (comprehension)
- Respond (to questions)
- Assess (text understanding)

Topics or Context:

Informational and literary texts, specifically _____

Big Ideas

Student-worded:

1. Reading strategies help us better understand whatever kind of reading we do.

2. Skilled readers can retell whatever they read in their own words and explain how it's the same and different from another selection.

3. Knowing how to ask and answer questions about our reading helps us understand it better.

4. Skilled readers can back up their predictions and conclusions with examples from their reading.

Essential Questions

1. What are reading strategies? Why do we need to learn them?

2. How do we share a story or information with someone else?

3. Why do we ask questions about whatever we read?

4. What are predictions and conclusions? How do we make them?

Concepts:	***Need to <u>Know</u> About <u>The Writing Process</u>***

Indiana Language Arts Standard 4

Building Stories
- Story ideas
- Pictures
- Letters
- Words

Writing Procedure
- Phonetically spelled words
- Consonant-vowel-consonant (CVC) words
- Left to right
- Top to bottom

Skills:	***Be Able to <u>Do</u>***

- Discuss (ideas)
- Tell (a story)
- Write (words)

Topics or Context:

- Thanksgiving
- 100 days
- Colors
- Getting to Know You

Big Ideas

1. Discussing ideas helps us to tell stories.

2. Telling a story includes pictures, letters, and words.

3. Sounding out words helps us to write stories.

Essential Questions

1. How do we get an idea for a story?

2. What do we need to tell a story?

3. Why do we need to sound out words?

[3] Reprinted with permission.

Concepts:	### Need to <u>Know</u> About <u>Writing</u>

Structure
- Conventions of writing
- Complete sentences
- Vocabulary
- Spelling

Meaning
- Descriptive words
- Sequencing
- Variety of writing forms
- Related sentences

Skills:	### Be Able to <u>Do</u>

- Write, dictate, draw
- Organize
- Edit
- Revise
- Publish
- Word process

Topics or Context:

Journaling, letter writing, reports, research, shared group writing, stories, book reports, assessments, labeling

Big Ideas

1. Good writing needs to follow a pattern.

2. A writer sequences, describes, and sticks to the topic.

3. A good writer pre-writes, writes, edits, and publishes.

Essential Questions

1. What is good writing?

2. How can you tell if your story has meaning?

3. What is the writing process? How do you use it?

Kindergarten – Grade 1
Jean Burns and Krista Stompanato[4]
Summit View Elementary
School District of Waukesha, Wisconsin

Concepts:

Need to __Know__ About __Writing__
Wisconsin Writing B. 4.1
Create or produce writing to communicate with different
audiences for a variety of purposes.

Communication/Message
- Share thoughts
- Share experiences
- Share opinions

Writing Purposes
- Nonfiction/Technical (messages, directions, details, facts, sequence of events)
- Expressive/Narrative (reflections, letters, details, personal voice)
- Creative (poetry, fiction, plays)

Audiences
- Self
- Parents
- Peers
- Teachers

Variety of Writing Situations
- Home
- School

Writing Strategies
- Adapt
- Brainstorm
- Use references

Writing Materials
- Pencils
- Crayons
- Paper
- Computer
- References

[4] Reprinted with permission.

(continued)

Skills: ***Be Able to <u>Do</u>***

- Identify (various writing purposes)
- Recognize (letters/sounds have meaning)
- Illustrate (message)
- Write (letters, words, phrases, sentences)
- Use materials (pencil, crayons, paper, computer, references)
- Apply (variety of situations/places)
- Revise
- Edit
- Discuss (messages)
- Explain (messages)
- Evaluate (messages/writings)

Topics or Context:

In addition to the performance task of writing a bug poem, the students will participate in the following activities:

- Journal writing
- Daily message
- Writing center
- Mini-lessons
- Interactive writing
- Language experience
- Interactive read-alouds
- Alphabet Center
- Poetry Center

Big Ideas

1. Writing communicates ideas.

2. Purpose determines the writing we choose.

3. Writers write to different audiences.

4. Writing is a part of everyday life.

Essential Questions

1. Why do we write? What kind of ideas do we write?

2. How do you know what to write?

3. Who is your audience? Why would you write to different people?

4. When do we use writing?

LANGUAGE ARTS — Reading
Grade 2
Wayne Township[5]
Indianapolis, Indiana

Concepts: ***Need to <u>Know</u> About <u>Writing Applications</u>***

Indiana Language Arts Standard 5

Narrative
- Sequence of events (personal experiences)
- Details of setting, characters, objects, events
- Descriptive words

Descriptive
- Main idea surrounding a noun (object, person, events, place)
- Supporting details
- Descriptive words

Friendly Letter
- Five parts (date, salutation, body, closing, signature)

Skills: ***Be Able to <u>Do</u>***

- Include (setting details and events)
- Move through (sequences)
- Describe (characters, objects)
- Develop (main idea)
- Use (details to support main idea)
- Develop (friendly letter including five parts)
- Distinguish (different purposes)

Topics or Context:

- Poems, rhymes
- Friendly letters
- Personal stories
- Timeline events

[5] Reprinted with permission.

(continued)

Big Ideas

1. To make sense, narratives need to move through a sequence of setting, characters, objects, and events.

2. Descriptive writing needs to include the main idea, supporting details, and descriptive words.

3. A friendly letter needs to include the five main parts written with descriptive words.

Essential Questions

1. What are story elements? Why do stories need to follow a sequence?

2. How is descriptive writing organized?

3. What are the parts of a friendly letter? Why is each one important?

Concepts:

Need to <u>Know</u> About <u>Writing Applications</u>
Indiana Writing Standard 5

Narratives (Fiction)
- Context for action
- Details to develop plot

Descriptive Pieces (Nonfiction)
- Unified main idea
- Supporting details
- People, places, things, experiences

Letters and Notes (Written Communication)
- Personal
- Persuasive
- Formal and informal
- Thank-you
- Invitations
- Appropriate format
- Audience and purpose
- Varied words

Skills:

Be Able to <u>Do</u>

- Provide (context)
- Include (details, appropriate format)
- Develop (plot, unified main idea)
- Use (details, writing process)
- Describe (familiar object, event, experience)
- Explain (familiar object, event, experience)
- Show (awareness)
- Establish (purpose)

Topics or Context:

- Short stories
- Letters and notes
- Nonfiction writing

(continued)

Big Ideas

1. Narratives (fictional writings) need a specific setting and supporting details to advance plot.

2. Descriptive (nonfiction) writing develops a main idea with supporting details.

3. Different kinds of writing communicate information for a variety of purposes and audiences.

Student-worded "Big Ideas"

1. Stories need a place to happen with details that keep readers interested.

2. The best fiction and nonfiction writing explains an idea completely.

3. Writers need to know how to communicate in different ways for different people.

Essential Questions

1. Why does every story need a setting?

2. Why are supporting details important in both fiction and nonfiction?

3. In what ways do writers communicate different kinds of information? How do writers know when to use each kind?

MATH
Grade 1, Standard 1[6]
Kristin Parisi
Chapelwood Elementary
Wayne Township
Indianapolis, Indiana

Concepts: ***Need to <u>Know</u> About <u>Number Sense</u>***

Number Sense
- Representing numbers using objects
- Matching objects and numbers

Skills: ***Be Able to <u>Do</u>***

- Count, Read, Write (whole numbers)
- Count and Group (objects)
- Identify (tens and ones)
- Name (one more and one less)
- Compare (whole numbers)
- Match (ordinal numbers)
- Recognize (congruent shapes)
- Describe (shaded portions)
- Represent (subsets)
- Write (fractions)
- Represent, Compare, Interpret (data)

Topics or Context:

- Mathematics textbook
- Everyday Counts
- Mountain Math
- TLC (Teaching and Learning with Computers) Stations

Big Idea

1. We have to understand numbers so that we can count and talk about numbers with other people.

Essential Question

1. Why do we have to understand numbers?

---

[6] Author's Note: Kristin Parisi of Chapelwood Elementary in Wayne Township, Indianapolis, Indiana, "unwrapped" for use in her own instructional program each of the six Indiana math standards for Grade 1. She generously consented to allow me to publish all six examples.

MATH
Grade 1, Standard 2

Concepts: ***Need to <u>Know</u> About <u>Computation</u>***

Computation
- Addition
- Subtraction

Skills: ***Be Able to <u>Do</u>***

- Show (addition, subtraction, equal numbers)
- Demonstrate (addition facts)
- Understand ($+$, $-$, and $=$; zero)
- Understand and use (inverse relationship)

Topics or Context:

- Mathematics textbook
- Everyday Counts
- Mountain Math
- TLC (Teaching and Learning with Computers) Stations
- Flash Cards
- Mad Minute Tests

Big Ideas

1. Addition is putting numbers or things together and subtraction is taking them away.

2. Addition and subtraction are opposites.

Essential Questions

1. What is addition? What is subtraction?

2. How are addition and subtraction related?

MATH
Grade 1, Standard 3

Concepts: ***Need to <u>Know</u> About <u>Algebra and Functions</u>***

Number Sentences and Problem Solving
- Word problems
- Addition and subtraction symbols

Skills: ***Be Able to <u>Do</u>***

- Write and solve (number sentences)
- Create (word problems)
- Recognize and use (addition and subtraction)
- Create and extend (number patterns)

Topics or Context:

- Mathematics textbook
- Everyday Counts
- Mountain Math
- TLC (Teaching and Learning with Computers) Stations
- Flash Cards
- Mad Minute Tests

Big Ideas

1. Number sentences are addition and subtraction sentences.

2. We solve number sentences by doing what the sentence tells us to do.

Essential Question

1. What are number sentences, and how do we solve them?

MATH
Grade 1, Standard 4

Concepts: ***Need to <u>Know</u> About <u>Geometry</u>***

Geometry
- Shapes
- Attributes
- Location

Skills: ***Be Able to <u>Do</u>***

- Identify, describe, compare, sort, and draw (triangles, rectangles, squares, and circles)
- Classify and sort (plane and solid objects)
- Identify (two- or three-dimensional objects; shapes and structures)
- Give and follow (directions)
- Arrange and describe (objects)

Topics or Context:

- Mathematics textbook
- Everyday Counts
- Mountain Math
- TLC (Teaching and Learning with Computers) Stations
- Flash Cards
- Mad Minute Tests
- Geoboards
- Pattern Blocks
- Attribute Blocks

Big Ideas

1. Shapes are the things that we see.

2. Shapes are alike and different from each other.

Essential Questions

1. What are shapes called? How are they related?

MATH
Grade 1, Standard 5

Concepts: ***Need to <u>Know</u> About <u>Measurement</u>***

- Length
- Compare
- Order
- Describe

Skills: ***Be Able to <u>Do</u>***

- Measure (length)
- Use (units of measurement)
- Recognize (fixed unit)
- Measure and estimate (length)
- Compare and order (objects)
- Tell (time)
- Identify and give (value of pennies, nickels, and dimes)

Topics or Context:

- Mathematics textbook
- Everyday Counts
- Mountain Math
- TLC (Teaching and Learning with Computers) Stations
- Flash Cards
- Mad Minute Tests
- Money
- Clocks

Big Ideas

1. Units of measurement are what we use to measure things, like inches, pennies, nickels, and dimes.

2. We use them to measure things and keep them in order.

Essential Question

1. What are units of measurement, and why do we use them?

MATH
Grade 1, Standard 6

Concepts: ***Need to <u>Know</u> About <u>Problem Solving</u>***

Set Up Problems
- Problem solving
- Model

Solve Problems and Reason
- Procedures and results
- Connections

Skills: ***Be Able to <u>Do</u>***

- Choose (approach, materials, and strategies)
- Use (tools)
- Explain (reasoning)
- Justify (procedures)
- Make (calculations)
- Check (validity)
- Understand and use (connections)

Topics or Context:

- Mathematics textbook
- Everyday Counts
- Mountain Math
- TLC (Teaching and Learning with Computers) Stations

Big Ideas

1. A story problem tells a story using words and numbers.

2. To solve a story problem you have to start with what you know and figure out what you don't know.

3. Then you have to write a number sentence to find the answer.

Essential Question

1. What is a story problem, and how do you solve it?

Concepts: ***Need to <u>Know</u> About <u>Mathematical Processes</u>***

Problem-Solving Strategies
- Discussion
- Own Words
- Diagrams
- Physical models
- Patterns
- Pictures

Solutions

Needed/Not Needed Information

Skills: ***Be Able to <u>Do</u>***
- Use (various strategies)
- Explain (solutions)
- Illustrate (solutions)
- Identify (needed/not needed information)

Topics or Context:
- Classroom problem-solving activities

Big Ideas

1. Many strategies are used to solve everyday problems.

2. A good problem solver determines which information is necessary to solve problems and which isn't.

3. A good problem solver recognizes when results don't make sense.

4. Solutions can be explained through writing and speaking.

Essential Questions

1. How can you solve everyday problems?

2. What information do you need to know in order to solve problems?

3. How do you know if your answer is reasonable?

4. How can you explain your solutions to problems?

[7] Reprinted with permission.

SOCIAL STUDIES
Grade 2
Anonymous

Concepts: ***Need to <u>Know</u> About <u>People Make a Difference</u>***

- History of family
- Extraordinary people
- Contemporary people
- Location of people, places, environments
- Geographical features

Skills: ***Be Able to <u>Do</u>***

- Locating
- Labeling
- Tracing
- Mapping
- Identifying
- Describing
- Sequencing
- Demonstrating
- Comparing
- Contrasting
- Researching

Topics or Context:

- Family History Timeline

Big Ideas

1. People's differences are a result of time, place, and resources.

2. Learning about people, places, and environment helps us understand our history.

3. Geography affects how we live.

Essential Questions

1. What causes people's differences?

2. How can we understand our own history?

3. Why don't all people live the same way and do the same things?

SOCIAL STUDIES
Grade 2
Deborah Hines, Jody Petersman, Jenny Powers, and Lisa Wampler[8]
Sharonville Elementary School, Princeton City Schools
Cincinnati, Ohio

Concepts: ***Need to <u>Know</u> About <u>Geography</u>***

Geographical Features
- Land Forms (mountains, valley, plain, desert, oasis, plateau, valley, horizon, peninsula, island)
- Continents (seven continents, Americas: North, Central, South)
- Bodies of Water (river, oceans, coast, lake)
- States (borders, boundaries)

Maps
- Equator
- Prime Meridian
- Hemispheres
- Locations
- Compass Rose
- Directions
- Regions
- Latitude and Longitude
- Key/Scale

Skills: ***Be Able to <u>Do</u>***

- Identify
- Describe
- Create
- Construct
- Use
- Locate
- Trace
- Compare
- Name
- Recognize
- Explain

Topics or Context:

- Grade 2 Geography Unit

[8] Reprinted with permission.   *(continued)*

Grade 2, Deborah Hines, Jody Petersman, Jenny Powers, and Lisa Wampler,
Sharonville Elementary School, Cincinnati, Ohio *(continued)*

Big Ideas

1. The Earth is made up of land formations and bodies of water.

2. You live on a continent, in a country, in a specific region, and in a state.

3. Maps help us find our place in the world.

Essential Questions

1. Which bodies of water and land formations make up the Earth?

2. Where in the world do you live, starting with the Earth and ending in your own state?

3. Why is a map important? What can you learn from it?

SCIENCE—Emphasizing IEP Goals for Language Arts
Kindergarten
Annette Kluge[9]
School District of Waukesha
Waukesha, Wisconsin

Concepts: ***Need to <u>Know</u> About <u>Insects</u>***

Prerequisite Knowledge/Skill: Understanding of same/different.

Vocabulary
- Egg
- Chrysalis
- Caterpillar
- Butterfly
- Wings
- Antennae
- Legs
- Body
- Monarch
- Milkweed
- Larva

Four Stages of Life Cycle
1. Egg
2. Caterpillar
3. Chrysalis
4. Butterfly

Skills: ***Be Able to <u>Do</u>***

- Describe (similarities/differences and life cycle stages)
- Observe (different stages of cycle and manipulatives/visuals)
- Identify (picture/sentence to match stage and similarities and differences)
- Gather and record data in journal (descriptions of stages)
- Retell/summarize (explain the life cycle)
- Recall facts and information

[9] Reprinted with permission.

(continued)

IEP Goals

1. Follow 2–4 step directions.

2. Listen without interrupting.

3. Speak in complete sentences.

4. Use correct speech sounds with appropriate volume.

5. Use appropriate listening behaviors (eyes on speaker and quiet hands).

6. Describe object using two or more attributes.

7. Stay on topic with relevant comments/questions.

8. Sequence four pictures.

Topics or Context:

- Books: *The Very Hungry Caterpillar* by Eric Carle; *Monarch Butterfly-Life Cycle* by David Schwartz; *Monarch Butterfly* by Gail Gibbons
- Journal writing of observations/match picture to indicate stage
- Jar with caterpillar and milkweed leaves
- Pictures of stages
- Pictures of caterpillar/butterfly and stuffed toy of caterpillar/butterfly
- Worksheets
- Ingredients for pretzel butterfly
- See music teacher to teach a butterfly song

Big Ideas

1. Animals have different body parts.

2. Animals move in different ways.

3. Some animals can change from one type of animal to another.

4. Animals are part of the environment.

Essential Questions

1. How are animals alike and different?

2. How do birds, fish, snakes, and elephants move?

3. How does a caterpillar change into a butterfly?

4. Where do caterpillars/butterflies live in the environment?

SCIENCE
Kindergarten
Kelly Flynn and Debbie Willett[10]
Sharonville Elementary
Princeton City School District
Cincinnati, Ohio

Concepts: ***Need to <u>Know</u> About <u>Plants and Plant Growth</u>***

Basic parts of a plant/Life cycle

What plants need to grow
- Air
- Food
- Light

Plants and seeds are used as food

Types of plants
- Deciduous
- Evergreen

George Washington Carver

Skills: ***Be Able to <u>Do</u>***
- Label
- Observe
- Record
- Classify
- Identify
- Sort
- Sequence
- Recall facts/information
- Interpret

Topics or Context:

- Planting
- Journal writing
- Experimenting
- Creating models
- Literature
- Drawing
- Songs

[10] Reprinted with permission.

(continued)

Big Ideas

1. Plants need air, food, and light to grow.

2. All plants have basic parts.

3. There are two types of plants. One type keeps its leaves all year long, the other one doesn't.

4. Plants and seeds can be used as food.

5. George Washington Carver helped farmers grow plants.

Essential Questions

1. What do plants need to survive? Why might a plant die?

2. What are the parts of a plant? Why are they important?

3. How are plants the same? How are they different?

4. How do we use plants?

5. Who was the famous scientist who helped farmers grow plants? How did he help you?

SCIENCE
Grade 2
Renee B. Rios and Joan T. Wagner[11]
South-West Park Elementary
Tracy Unified
Tracy, California

Concepts: ***Need to <u>Know</u> About <u>Growth and Change in Living Things</u>***
California Standards 2 c, e, f and 4 a, c, d

Categorizing Differences
- Living
  - Compare characteristics
  - Growth
  - Needs
- Nonliving
  - Compare characteristics
- Environment
  - Effects on growth
  - Cause and effect

Life Cycle
- Plants
- Seeds (sequence of change and growth)
- Animals
- Eggs (sequence of change and growth)

Scientific Process
1. Question (state purpose)

2. Prediction (make predictions based on prior observations and known patterns)

3. Investigation/Observation (recognize cause and effect)

4. Conclusion (restate facts and organize ideas based on comparisons made to prediction)

---

[11] Reprinted with permission.

(continued)

Grade 2, Renee B. Rios and Joan T. Wagner, South-West Park Elementary, Tracy Unified, Tracy, California *(continued)*

Skills:	***Be Able to <u>Do</u>***

- Recognize (differences between living and nonliving things)
- Identify (characteristics of living and nonliving things)
- Understand (factors that influence growth in living things—cause and effect)
- Identify (stages of growth process)
- Make (scientific predictions based on prior observations)
- Restate (facts and details based on comparisons and observations)

Topics or Context:

- Harcourt Science, Unit A/Ch. 1/Lessons 1–3
- Prior knowledge (assess what they know)
- Graphic organizers (K-W-L chart, flow chart, Venn diagram)
- Introduction to vocabulary
- Lab Activity (seed experiment and leaf classification)
- Realia (plants, flowers, fruit, people), picture cards
- Cooperative learning
- Scientific journals (applying comprehension and writing strategies)

Big Ideas

1. Living things change as they grow.

2. Offspring look like their parents in many ways.

3. You can group objects when they look the same.

4. Plants grow from seeds that come from flowers and fruits.

Essential Questions

1. What types of change can we see when things grow?

2. How do offspring look like their parents?

3. When and how can we group objects together?

4. How do seeds grow?

PHYSICAL EDUCATION
Kindergarten – Grade 4

(Please see last example in Chapter Six)

Upper Elementary Standards "Unwrapped"

In this chapter dedicated to the upper elementary grades, 3 or 4 through 5, I have included numerous examples of "unwrapped" standards and indicators from several content areas, particularly language arts, mathematics, science, and social studies. You may also wish to review the primary grade examples in the previous chapter and the middle grade examples in the next chapter. Many of these may be adaptable to upper elementary grades.

These "unwrapped" examples were created by me and by seminar participants in different states. I have received permission from these educators to reprint their work for the publication of this book. A few of the examples included were submitted anonymously during the guided practice "unwrapping" activity at the seminar.

Please note: I have not included the full text of the standards and indicators along with the graphic organizer of "unwrapped" concepts and skills. Although inclusion of the full text would indeed have been helpful, particularly for educators in the individual states from which the "unwrapped" standards originate, printing limitations made this infeasible. Certain examples do identify particular states and standards, however.

Lastly, a few of the graphic organizers do not include parenthetical "targets" after the skills. The educators involved either chose not to include them, or they attended one of my earlier "unwrapping" standards seminars where I did not emphasize their importance to the degree that I do now.

The central purpose for including these examples is to provide readers with a wide variety of graphic organizers, Big Ideas, and Essential Questions in several content areas that they can reference to more fully comprehend the "unwrapping" process. To all those who have generously contributed to this collection of examples, I thank you on behalf of all educators whose understanding of how to "unwrap" will deepen as a result of your work.

LANGUAGE ARTS
Elementary
Author

Concepts: ***Need to <u>Know</u> about <u>Literary Response</u> <u>and Expression</u>***

New York Standard 2

- Imaginative texts

- Social, historical, cultural features

- Literary merit

- Comprehension strategies
  - Inference
  - Deduction
  - Phonics
  - Context cues

- Different genres
  - (Picture books)
  - Fiction
  - Nonfiction
  - Poems
  - Articles (and stories)
  - Fables
  - Myths
  - Legends
  - Plays
  - Media productions

- Literary elements
  - Setting
  - Character
  - Plot
  - Theme
  - Point of view

Skills: ***Be Able to <u>Do</u>***

- Comprehend (imaginative texts in every medium)
- Interpret (imaginative texts in every medium)
- Critique (imaginative texts in every medium)
- Draw on (personal experiences)
- Recognize (social, cultural, historical features)
- Read (variety of literature in different genres)
- Recognize (genre features)
- Use (features to comprehend)

(continued)

- Understand (literary elements)
- Compare (elements to other works, own lives)
- Use (inference and deduction)
- Read aloud (accurately, fluently)
- Use (phonics, context cues)
- Evaluate (literary merit)

Topics or Context:

- Picture books
- Class anthology of favorite poems
- Reading inventory (of literature read)
- Fairy tales and fables (myths and legends)
- Songs, plays, media productions
- Self-selected books (fiction and nonfiction)

Big Ideas

1. All works of fiction use the same literary elements in different ways.

2. Writers express their ideas and imagination in different formats depending on their purpose and personal choice.

3. The value of literature is directly related to its representation of society, history, and culture.

4. Skilled readers use specific strategies to better understand what they read.

Essential Questions

1. How is fiction organized to tell a story?

2. What are genres of literature? How do authors use them?

3. What makes writing "literature"?

4. How can readers improve their reading abilities?

LANGUAGE ARTS
End of Grade 4
Author

Concepts:

Need to <u>Know</u> about <u>End of Grade 4 Reading Comprehension</u>

New Jersey Literacy Standard 3.4

- Types of understanding
  - Literal
  - Inference
  - Deduction

- Print concepts

- Facts, personal opinion, point of view

- Elements of story
  - Setting
  - Character
  - Sequence of events

- Literary forms
  - Fiction
  - Poetry
  - Drama
  - Nonfiction

- Strategies and techniques
  - Word analysis
  - Context clues

Skills:

Be Able to <u>Do</u>

- Read (independently, literally, inferentially, critically, with comprehension)
- Use (print concepts; prior knowledge)
- Link (aspects of text to personal lives)
- Identify (point-of-view in text)
- Distinguish (author opinion and point-of-view; fact vs. fiction)
- Demonstrate (comprehension)
- Retell/summarize (ideas)
- Follow (written directions)
- Identify (story elements; literature forms)
- Expand (vocabulary)
- Read/use (variety of print materials)

(continued)

Topics or Context:

- "Variety of lit from authors of different cultures, ethnicities, genders, and ages" (excerpted verbatim from New Jersey standards)
- Nonfiction materials (technical manuals, print material from other subject areas)

Big Ideas

1. Understanding what we read in different ways helps us develop our own opinion and point of view.

2. All works of literature use the same elements to effectively tell a complete story.

3. Authors use particular forms of writing according to their purpose and personal choice.

Essential Questions

1. Is there more than one way to understand what we read?

2. What are literary elements? Why do authors use them?

3. Why do all authors choose to express their ideas the way they do?

LANGUAGE ARTS
Grades 3–5
Oakwood Schools[1]
Ohio

Concepts: **Need to <u>Know</u> About <u>Reading Comprehension Strategies</u>**

Comprehension Strategies
- Summaries
- Predictions
- Comparisons
- Responses
- Self-monitoring

Purpose for Reading

Applications across Subject Areas

Skills: **Be Able to <u>Do</u>**

- Summarize
- Predict
- Compare
- Contrast
- Respond
- Self-monitor
- Establish (purpose for reading)
- Apply (comprehension strategies across subject matter areas)

Topics or Context:

- Grade-level appropriate novels and nonfiction reading materials

Big Ideas

1. People read for many different purposes.

2. Readers use specific strategies to comprehend what they read.

3. Readers extract meaning from the text.

4. Readers use self-monitoring strategies to maintain their understanding.

Essential Questions

1. Why do people read?

2. How do readers understand what they read?

3. What is the purpose of reading?

4. What do readers do to maintain comprehension throughout the reading process?

[1] Reprinted with permission.

LANGUAGE ARTS
Grades 3–4
Diane McCarroll, Karen Winchester, and Beth Wyandt[2]
Englewood Elementary
Northmont School District
Englewood, Ohio

Concepts: ***Need to <u>Know</u> About <u>Writing Applications</u>***

Narrative Accounts
- Character
- Setting
- Plot

Responses to Literature
- Main idea and significant details
- Interpretations
- References

Formal and Informal Letters
- Correct letter format

Informational Reports
- Facts, details, and examples

Skills: ***Be Able to <u>Do</u>***

- Write (narrative accounts, responses to literature, formal and informal letters, informational reports)
- Develop (character, setting, plot)
- Summarize (main idea, significant details)
- Support (interpretations with reference to text)
- Include (important details, facts, examples)
- Follow (correct letter format)
- Illustrate (important ideas)

Topics or Context:

- (To Be Decided)

Big Ideas

1. Good writers can write in different forms depending on the assignments (fiction or nonfiction).

2. Good writers include important details to support their main ideas.

Essential Questions

1. Why do we use different forms of writing?

2. How can good writers support their main ideas?

---

[2] Reprinted with permission.

LANGUAGE ARTS
Grade 5
Anonymous

Concepts: ***Need to <u>Know</u> About <u>Writing Applications</u>***

Narratives
- Story elements (setting, character, plot, climax)
- Events of story (beginning, conflict, resolution)

Responses to Literature
- Understanding of literary work
- Support opinion (references and prior knowledge)
- Personal responses

Research Report
- Direct investigation
- Main ideas
- Variety of sources
- Topic development (details, simple facts, examples)

Persuasive Letters and Compositions
- Taking a position
- Supporting position with evidence and emotion
- Organizational patterns
- Related concerns

Skills: ***Be Able to <u>Do</u>***

- Establish (plot, story elements)
- Show (events of story)
- Demonstrate (comprehension)
- Develop (interpretations)
- Support (judgments, point of view)
- Organize (information)
- Read
- Evaluate
- Identify
- Respond
- Research
- Analyze

Topics or Context:

- In-depth research of theme
- Literature responses
- Articles (news/editorials)

(continued)

Big Ideas

1. All narratives need sequential story elements that focus on conflict and resolution.

2. References, prior knowledge, and understanding of literary work can support personal opinions in one's own written work.

3. Research reports show the development of a topic through investigation using a variety of resources.

4. Persuasive compositions support positions through evidence and emotions in a convincing tone.

Essential Questions

1. How does an author build a story to reach a powerful climax and resolution?

2. What strategies support your personal opinions?

3. Why do we do research?

4. How do you persuade someone to share your opinion?

Concepts: ***Need to <u>Know</u> About <u>End of Grade 4 Number Sense</u>***
New Jersey Math Standard 4.6

- Whole numbers
- Fractions
- Decimals
- Place value and numeration
- Number sequences and patterns
- Extensions of number system
- Uses of numbers
    - Counting
    - Measuring
    - Labeling
    - Indicating location
- Equivalent forms
- Negative numbers

Skills: ***Be Able to <u>Do</u>***

- Construct (number meaning)
- Understand (place value, numeration, extension of number system, number uses)
- See (patterns)
- Use (pattern-based thinking; models)
- Develop (sense of magnitude)
- Count/perform (money computations)
- Relate (numbers to each other)
- Represent (equivalent forms)
- Compare and order (numbers)
- Explore (real-life settings)

Topics or Context:

- "Real-life experiences, physical materials, and technology" (excerpted verbatim from New Jersey standards)

(continued)

Big Ideas

1. The place of a digit determines its value.

2. Fractions and decimals represent values less than, equal to, or greater than one whole.

3. Numbers are tools to help us measure, label, count, and sequence.

4. Different numbers can have the same value.

5. Numbers can be expanded when you see the pattern for doing so.

Essential Questions

1. What determines the value of a number?

2. How are numbers "tools"?

3. How can numbers be both different and the same?

4. How can we build bigger numbers?

MATH
Grade 4
Kathy Callahan, Leslie Guzulaitis, Annie Chudzynski, Melissa Smith, Paula Frederick, Cynthia Coapstick, and Mark Mull[3]
Chapel Glen Elementary and Robey Elementary
Metropolitan School District of Wayne Township
Indianapolis, Indiana

Concepts:

Need to <u>Know</u> About <u>Data Analysis and Probability</u>
Grade 4 Indiana Math Standard 6

Data Representations
- Number line
- Tables
- Frequency tables
- Graphs
- Numerical and categorical

Skills:

Be Able to <u>Do</u>

- Organize, represent, and interpret (data)
- Communicate (findings)
- Show (outcomes for probability situations)
- Summarize and display (results of probability experiments)
- Answer (questions about a situation)

Topics or Context:

- Data (surveys)
- Tables, charts, graphs
- Technology
- Graphic organizers for data
- Real-life situations

Big Ideas

1. Number lines, data graphs, and tables clearly represent categorical data.

2. By using the words "most," "some," and "few," graph patterns can be described (interpreted) clearly.

Essential Questions

1. How can categorical data be shown in a clear way?

2. How is a graph described/interpreted clearly?

[3] Reprinted with permission.

MATH
Grade 5
Arlisa Kirton and Tony Flach[4]
Campostella Elementary and James Monroe Elementary
Norfolk Public Schools
Norfolk, Virginia

Concepts:	***Need to <u>Know</u> About <u>Algebra</u>***

Virginia Standards of Learning 5.20 and 5.21

Concept of a Variable
- Symbol standing for any one of a set of numbers or objects
- A quantity that can change

Verbal Quantitative Expression
- Use numbers when quantities are known
- Use variables when quantities are unknown
- Expression can be a number, a variable, or show an operation with a number and a variable

Open Sentences
- A mathematical sentence with a variable and an equal sign

Problem Situation
- A scenario incorporating open sentences with a single variable and a number

Skills: ***Be Able to <u>Do</u>***
- Investigate (the concept of a variable)
- Describe (the concept of a variable)
- Use (a variable)
- Represent (a verbal quantitative expression)
- Write (open sentences)
- Create (problem situations)

Topics or Context:
- "Cater a Party" Algebra-based Performance Assessment

Big Ideas

1. Algebra solves real-life problems when numbers are unknown.

2. Variables change value because they represent different quantities.

Essential Questions

1. How can algebra help us solve real-life problems?

2. How and why does the value of a variable change?

[4] Reprinted with permission.

SCIENCE
Grade 4
Lori Burkhart[5]
Fairlawn Elementary
Norfolk Public Schools
Norfolk, Virginia

Concepts: ***Need to <u>Know</u> About <u>Energy and Motion</u>***

Energy Forms
- Electrical
- Mechanical
- Chemical

States of Energy
- Potential
- Kinetic

Machines
- Simple
  - Lever
  - Wheel and axle
  - Pulley
  - Screw
  - Wedge
  - Inclined plane
- Compound

Energy-Related Vocabulary
- Efficiency
- Friction
- Inertia

Skills: ***Be Able to <u>Do</u>***
- Explain and demonstrate (work being done, energy needed to do work, inertia)
- Differentiate (potential and kinetic)
- Determine (energy form, effect of friction on moving objects)
- Describe (simple machines and functions)
- Identify (simple machines in compound machines)
- Analyze (common household items for a simple machine)
- Design (investigations)
- Show (machines make work easier)
- Give (examples of simple machines)

Topics or Context:

- (To be decided)

[5] Reprinted with permission.

(continued)

Big Ideas

1. Energy can change forms, but never disappears.

2. Forces such as friction can affect motion and work by making them more difficult to carry out.

3. Machines make our work easier and more efficient.

4. All matter in motion can resist change.

Essential Questions

1. Does the energy in a roller coaster ride disappear when the ride is over?

2. How does friction affect work and motion?

3. What are the six simple machines? How do they help us?

4. How does inertia affect the motions of objects?

SCIENCE
Grade 4
V. Gill, P. Swingle, P. Saunders, and Bill O'Connell[6]
MRSD
New Hampshire

Concepts: ***Need to <u>Know</u> About <u>the Circle of Life</u>***
"Unwrapped" Standards from Science, Social Studies, Language Arts, Math

- Producers and Consumers
- Predators and Prey
- Herbivores, Carnivores, Omnivores
- Food Chain and Food Web
- Habitat
- Interdependence
- Decomposers
- Adaptations
- Ecosystems
- Competition
- Energy
- Cycles
- Population

Skills: ***Be Able to <u>Do</u>***

- Classify (animals)
- Identify (adaptations)
- List (members of food chain)
- Explain (likenesses/differences herbivore, carnivore, omnivore)
- Write (information)
- Communicate (ideas and facts)
- Research
- Analyze and apply (data)

Topics or Context:

- Poster
- Diagram
- Report
- Food Web
- Model

[6] Reprinted with permission.

(continued)

Big Ideas

1. Plants and animals are members of food chains that get their energy from the sun.

2. Animals have adaptations that help them survive.

3. New Hampshire plants and animals live in different ecosystems.

4. Animals in a community are interdependent.

Essential Questions

1. How is the sun's energy transferred to all living things?

2. Why are animals so different from one another? How do they survive?

3. How is New Hampshire's environment suitable to the animals that live there?

4. What if a member of a food chain was eliminated?

SCIENCE
Grade 4
Anonymous

Concepts: ***Need to <u>Know</u> About <u>Life Science</u>***

Basic Needs of Living Things
- Living vs. nonliving
- Adaptations
- Effects of environmental change
- Care of living things

Reactions of Organisms to Change
- Population changes
- Individual changes
- Regular vs. irregular changes
- Advantages and disadvantages of changes

Skills: ***Be Able to <u>Do</u>***
- Identify
- Distinguish
- Discuss
- Demonstrate
- Explain
- Compare

Topics or Context:

- Real-world examples
- Hands-on labs

Big Ideas

1. All organisms have the same set of life characteristics.

2. Organisms adapt so that they can survive under varying conditions.

3. All organisms must meet certain needs in order to stay alive.

Essential Questions

1. What makes something alive? Can you think of a non-living thing that has life characteristics?

2. What is an environmental change? How do organisms react to these changes?

3. What are the basic needs of living things? Why can some organisms survive in an environment and others cannot?

HISTORY/SOCIAL SCIENCE
Grade 4
Anonymous

Concepts: ***Need to <u>Know</u> About <u>Revolutionary War</u> <u>and Its Impact on Our State</u>***

Revolutionary War
- Key individuals
- Key events
- Relationships
- Timelines

Our State's Development
- Key individuals
- Key events
- Relationships
- Timelines

Skills: ***Be Able to <u>Do</u>***

- Organize (timelines that show relationships)
- Interpret (timelines)
- Explain (importance and influences of key events and people)

Topics or Context:

- Study of Revolutionary War and our state's history

Big Ideas

1. There are similarities in the growth of our nation and the growth of our state.

2. Key people and events at the national level influence what happens at the state level.

Essential Questions

1. What do you know about the Revolutionary War? What was its impact on our state?

2. What is the relationship between the federal government and our state?

INFORMATION AND TECHNOLOGY LITERACY
Grade 4
Mary Beth Haas, Marilyn Koehnlein, and Katie Kraemer[7]
School District of Waukesha
Waukesha, Wisconsin

Concepts:

Need to <u>Know</u> About <u>Research and Presentation</u>
Wisconsin Information and Technology Literacy Standards
A.4.5, B.4.1, B.4.2, B.4.4, B.4.5, B.4.7, B.4.8

Problem
- Ask the question

Media and Technology
- Keyboarding, graphics

Information-Seeking Strategies
- Problem

Variety of Materials
- Print, nonprint, electronic

Information
- Ideas, concepts

Communication
- Audience
- Ideas
- Written, oral, visual

Presentation Format
- Storyboard
- PowerPoint

Skills:

Be Able to <u>Do</u>

- Formulate (question)
- Locate (appropriate materials)
- Select (from a variety of resources)
- Match (materials to student ability)
- Research (topic)
- Read (information)
- Take (notes) and record (main ideas)
- Organize (information into outline or storyboard form)
- Plan (pages of storyboard)
- Create (PowerPoint presentation)
- Review and evaluate (final product)
- Share (final product)

[7] Reprinted with permission.

(continued)

Topics or Context:

- Activities and lessons to develop research and note-taking skills

- PowerPoint as a teaching tool

Big Ideas

1. Technology is a tool that can be used to express ideas.

2. Reading is the key to unraveling new ideas.

3. Storyboards can be used to organize ideas.

4. Sharing information enables everyone to learn.

Essential Questions

1. How do we use technology to communicate?

2. Why do we read and research? How can ideas expand our knowledge?

3. What is a storyboard? How and why do we use storyboards?

4. How and why do people share information?

PHYSICAL EDUCATION
Kindergarten – Grade 4
Susie Wyrick[8]
Blair Elementary School
Waukesha School District
Waukesha, Wisconsin

Concepts:

Need to <u>Know</u> About <u>Elementary Physical Fitness</u>

Affective Domain

Enjoying physical activity (D.4.1)
- Fitness games
- Exposure to lead-up games
- Cooperative games unit

Acceptance of students' skills and abilities (G.4.2)
- Partner activities
- Group activities
- Cooperative games unit

Cognitive Domain

Moderate to vigorous physical activities (A.4.3)
- Running
- Biking
- Cross country skiing
- In-line skating
- Basketball
- Soccer
- Snow shoeing

Healthful benefits from regular physical activity (A.4.2)
- Muscular strength
- Cardiovascular endurance
- Flexibility
- Agility
- Speed
- Balance
- Better health

Identify components of physical fitness (E.4.1)
- Muscular strength (chin-ups, push-ups, sit-ups, vertical climb bars)
- Flexibility (quadriceps stretch, hamstring stretch, sit and reach, hurdler's stretch)
- Cardiovascular endurance (running, biking, skating, walking)
- Agility (tag games, shuttle run, lead-up games)
- Speed (100-yard dash, shuttle run, jumping rope)
- Balance (balance boards, balance beam, scales, tumbling unit)

[8] Reprinted with permission.

(continued)

Personal strengths and weaknesses (E.4.3)
- Fitness journal

Psychomotor Domain

Select and participate regularly in physical activity (A.4.1)
- Individual sports
- Team sports

Improving skills
- Skill work in individual sports
- Skill work in team sports

Maintaining good health
- Staying active

Skills:

Be Able to <u>Do</u>

- Experience (fitness games, lead-up games, and cooperative games unit)
- Demonstrate (acceptance of skills and abilities, and verbal and nonverbal behaviors)
- Identify (moderate and vigorous physical activities)
- Describe (strength, endurance, flexibility, agility, speed, balance, and better health)
- Identify (muscular strength, flexibility, cardiovascular endurance, agility, and speed)
- Describe (strengths and weakness)
- Elevate (weaknesses to strengths)
- Select and participate (individual sports and team sports)

Topics or Context:

- Fitness games
- Lead-up games
- Cooperative games unit
- Partner activities
- Group activities
- Brainstorm as a class on moderate to vigorous physical activities.
- Students brainstorm in their fitness journals physical activities they enjoy doing
- Fitness testing unit
- Team sports
- Individual sports
- Bulletin board concept of the muscular system and cardiovascular system
- Fitness journal

(continued)

Big Ideas

1. Learning to select appropriate physical activities can be very enjoyable.

2. Physical activity has many health benefits.

3. Skill development promotes self-esteem and self-confidence.

4. Accepting other students' abilities and skills creates a positive and enjoyable environment for all.

Essential Questions

1. How can you select appropriate physical activities?

2. Why is physical activity important?

3. Why is it important to develop skills in physical education class?

4. Why is it important to encourage your classmates and give them positive feedback?

CHAPTER SEVEN

Middle School Standards "Unwrapped"

In this chapter dedicated to the middle school grades, 6 through 8, I have included numerous examples of "unwrapped" standards and indicators from several content areas, particularly language arts, mathematics, science, and social studies. You may also wish to review the upper elementary examples in the previous chapter and the high school examples in the next chapter. Many of these may be adaptable to middle school grades.

These "unwrapped" examples were created by me and by seminar participants in different states. I have received permission from these educators to reprint their work for the publication of this book. A few of the examples included were submitted anonymously during the guided practice "unwrapping" activity at the seminar.

Please note: I have not included the full text of the standards and indicators along with the graphic organizer of "unwrapped" concepts and skills. Although inclusion of the full text would indeed have been helpful, particularly for educators in the individual states from which the "unwrapped" standards originate, printing limitations made this infeasible. Certain examples do identify particular states and standards, however.

Lastly, a few of the graphic organizers do not include parenthetical "targets" after the skills. The educators involved either chose not to include them, or they attended one of my earlier "unwrapping" standards seminars where I did not emphasize their importance to the degree that I do now.

The central purpose for including these examples is to provide readers with a wide variety of graphic organizers, Big Ideas, and Essential Questions in several content areas that they can reference to more fully comprehend the "unwrapping" process. To all those who have generously contributed to this collection of examples, I thank you on behalf of all educators whose understanding of how to "unwrap" will deepen as a result of your work.

LANGUAGE ARTS — Integrated Reading and Writing
Grades 7–8
Melissa Coons and Julie Volbers[1]
Ben Davis Junior High School
MSD Wayne Township
Indianapolis, Indiana

Concepts: ***Need to <u>Know</u> About <u>Grade 7 READING</u>***

General Concepts
- Word Meaning
- Text Analysis
- Circumstances Surrounding Events

Literary Concepts
- Cause-and-Effect
- Plot
- Foreshadowing

Concepts: ***Need to <u>Know</u> About <u>Grade 7 WRITING</u>***

General Concepts
- Composition Structure
  - Transitions
  - Cohesiveness
  - Purpose
  - Style
  - Tone
- Capitalization
- Listening and Speaking
  - Organization of Thoughts
  - Effective Examples

Skills: ***Be Able to <u>Do</u>***

- Create (organizational structure)
- Use (transitions)
- Combine (ideas)
- Write (for different purposes)
- Capitalize (correctly)
- Speak (with precision)

Big Ideas

1. Cause-and-effect is one way that authors organize text.

2. All events in a story, present, past, and future, play a strategic part in its conclusion.

3. Authors use definitions, examples, and restatements to clarify word meanings.

[1] Reprinted with permission.   *(continued)*

Essential Questions

1. How does the organization of the text affect how well you understand the meaning?

2. What are the events surrounding plot that lead to the conclusion?

3. How does the author encourage vocabulary development?

Concepts: ***Need to Know About Grade 8 READING***

General Concepts
- Literal Word Meanings
- Figurative Word Meanings
- Literary Devices
  - Idioms
  - Analogies
  - Metaphors
  - Similes
  - Symbolism
  - Dialect
  - Irony

Reading Concepts
- Main Idea
- Details
- Underlying Meaning
- Summary

Skills: ***Be Able to Do***
- Analyze (figurative language)
- Infer (meanings of phrases)
- Compare (original text to summary)
- Identify (literary devices)

Topics or Context:
- Novels
- Short Story
- Performance Assessment
- Poetry
- Other Literary Works

(continued)

Concepts: ***Need to Know About Grade 8 WRITING***

Writing Process
- Thesis Statement
- Well-supported Conclusion
- Varied Sentence Types
  - Simple
  - Compound
  - Complex
  - Compound/Complex

Writing Applications
- Biographies
- Autobiographies
- Short Stories

Listening and Speaking
- Research Presentation

Skills: ***Be Able to Do***

- Create (compositions)
- Use (detail)
- Reveal (significance of subject)
  - Dialogue
  - Specific action
  - Physical description
  - Background description
- Compare/Contrast (characters)

Big Ideas

1. Authors use figurative devices to convey meaning.

2. An author defines his style through the use of literary devices.

3. An accurate summary of original text includes details and implies the same meaning.

Essential Questions

1. How does the author infer meaning in his writing?

2. What does the writer use to convey his style?

3. How do the summary and original text compare?

LANGUAGE ARTS—Writing
Grade 7
Anonymous

Concepts: ***Need to <u>Know</u> About <u>Editing and Revision</u>***

Editing Checklist
- Capitalization
- Punctuation
- Spelling
- Complete sentences
- Consistent verb tense
- Subject-verb agreement
- Standard English

Revision
- Word choice/precision of vocabulary
- Clarity
- Unity/cohesion
- Organization/logical flow of ideas

Skills: ***Be Able to <u>Do</u>***
- Write
- Review
- Revise/organize/improve
- Check
- Edit
- Proofread
- Evaluate (with scoring guide)

Topics or Context:
- Student writing (fiction and nonfiction)
- Peer writing and evaluation
- Teacher examples and modeling

Big Ideas

1. Editing skills address the mechanics of writing; revision skills address the content and organization of writing.

2. Both editing and revision skills are necessary for proficient writing.

3. Effective writers view writing as a continuous process of reflection and revision.

Essential Questions

1. What is the difference between editing and revising? How do writers utilize each of these?

2. How do effective writers produce an excellent piece of writing?

3. Why do writers continually rewrite?

Grade 8
Darin Willett and Sharon Melcher[2]
Sequoia School
Manteca Unified School District
Manteca, California

Concepts: ***Need to <u>Know</u> About <u>Oral Language — Speaking</u> <u>Strategies</u>***
California Speaking Applications Standard 2.1

Narrative Presentation (Biography)
- Event/Incident/Life Situation
- Significance of Subject's Attitude
- Narrative/Descriptive Strategies
  - relevant dialogue
  - physical description
  - specific action
  - background description
  - compare/contrast

Skills: ***Be Able to <u>Do</u>***

- Deliver (speech to peers)
- Relate (subject's thoughts to a specific audience)
- Reveal (factual information)
- Use (research skills to create biographical sketch)
- Employ (effective interview skills)

Topics or Context:

- Autobiographical Sketch
- Interview Skills
- Biographical Sketch
- Public Speaking

Big Ideas (Teacher-worded)

1. Good oral communicators present a coherent narrative to reach a specific audience for a specific purpose.

2. Good oral communicators demonstrate an understanding of their audience and utilize various media support to maintain interest.

3. An effective storyteller holds you captive. **(Student-worded)**

[2] Reprinted with permission.

(continued)

Essential Questions (Teacher-worded)

1. What speaking and presentation skills are vital to effectively communicate with your peers?

2. How do good interview and writing skills contribute to an effective multimedia presentation?

3. When sharing information with others, how are you presenting information that is meaningful and relevant to the audience?

Essential Questions (Student-worded)

1. What makes your story worth telling?

2. As a speaker, why do you need to know your audience?

3. What elements of a biography are necessary to capture a person's life?

4. How can you combine content and technology to effectively tell your story?

Concepts: ***Need to <u>Know</u> About <u>Number Sense and Operations</u>***
End of Grades 5 –7 Ohio Benchmarks

- Number line
- Numbers less than zero
- Number system properties for computations
- Fractions, decimals, integers
- Percents
  - Greater than 100
  - Less than 1
- Ratio and proportion
- Order of operations
  - Parentheses
  - Exponents
- Factors and multiples
  - Prime factorizations
  - Common factors
  - Common multiples
- Standard and nonstandard algorithms
- Proportional reasoning
- Multi-step problems

Skills: ***Be Able to <u>Do</u>***

- Represent/Compare (numbers less than zero)
- Extend (number line)
- Compare/Order/Convert (fractions, decimals, percents)
- Develop (meaning for percents)
- Use (models, pictures, order of operations, parentheses, exponents, proportional reasoning)
- Relate (ratio, proportion, percent)
- Solve (multi-step problems)
- Verify/Interpret (problem results)
- Apply (number system properties)
- Explain (prime factors, common factors, common multiples)
- Analyze (steps in standard/nonstandard algorithms)
- Estimate/Compute (integers, fractions, decimals, percents)

Topics or Context:

- Familiar applications (real-life situations) that involve multi-step problems

(continued)

Big Ideas

1. Number sense means understanding the relationships between numbers.

2. Fractions, decimals, and percents can represent the same amount differently.

3. Whether we estimate or compute the exact answer depends on the needs of the situation.

4. The different math formulas, algorithms, strategies, and skills are all tools to simplify the problem-solving process.

Essential Questions

1. What is number sense? How can we use it to solve mathematical problems?

2. What is the relationship between fractions, decimals, and percents?

3. When do we estimate? When do we need the exact answer?

4. Why learn math formulas and algorithms? How can they help us in real life?

Concepts: ***Need to <u>Know</u> About <u>Measurement</u>***
Indiana Math Standard 5

General Measurement Terms
- Length
- Area
- Volume
- Weight
- Time, money, temperatures
- Different angles
- Decimal notation

Circle Terms
- Ratio
- Constant pi
- Circumference
- Diameter
- Formulas
- Area of circles
- Estimates of pi (3.14 and 22/7)

Standard Units of Measurement
- Yards and square yards
- Miles and square miles
- Acres
- Fahrenheit

Metric Units of Measurement
- Meter and square meter
- Kilometer and square kilometer
- Celsius

Plane and Solid Shapes
- Significant figures
- Cube
- Rectangular box
- Two-dimensional patterns
- Surface area
- Right prisms
- Cylinders

(continued)

Skills: **Be Able to <u>Do</u>**

(Ideally, Verb Targets should be added from standards text for greater clarity)

- Know
- Understand
- Select
- Use
- Apply
- Solve
- Calculate
- Compare
- Estimate
- Round
- Construct
- Compute
- Convert
- Add, subtract, multiply, divide

Topics or Context:

- Measurement unit
- Problem-solving activities
- Real-life applications

Big Ideas

1. Knowledge and application of common measurement terms are necessary life skills.

2. Mathematical formulas and estimates both provide shortcuts for determining needed mathematical information.

3. Standard and metric units of measurement can be used interchangeably.

4. Measurement strategies and tools can be used to solve problems involving geometric shapes.

Essential Questions

1. Why do we need to know and be able to use common measurement terms?

2. Why learn mathematical formulas? How do estimation and formulas work together?

3. What is the relationship between standard and metric units of measurement? How are both used in today's world?

4. How can measurement strategies help us in situations involving geometry?

ALGEBRA I
Josh Peretti[3]
Carr Intermediate School
Santa Ana Unified School District
Santa Ana, California

Concepts:

Need to _Know_ About _Equations and Inequalities_

California Standards 3.0 through 9.0

One Variable
- Opposite operations
- Properties
- Absolute values
- Simplify

Two Variables
- Slope
- X and Y intercepts
- Graph and sketch
- Point-slope formula
- Parallel and perpendicular lines and their slopes
- System of equations/inequalities
  - Solving algebraically
  - Solving graphically

Skills:

Be Able to _Do_

- Solve/Isolate (variables)
- Graph/Sketch
- Compute (intercepts)
- Derive (point-slope, slope-intercept)
- Understand
- Interpret

Topics or Context:

Real-World Problems
- Word problems that require writing equations
- Systems of equations that compare different rates of change (phone plans, lightbulb life, etc.)

---

[3] Reprinted with permission.

(continued)

Big Ideas

1. Linear equations can explain real-life situations.

2. Algebraic solutions can be visualized on graphs.

3. There are precise and systematic ways to solve both inequalities and linear equations.

Essential Questions

1. What are linear equations? How can we use them in real life?

2. What information can one derive from the graph of an equation or inequality?

3. How do we solve linear equations and inequalities?

ALGEBRA I
Rick Fair, Gary Emmert, Carol Robison, Sheila Johnston, and Sue Humphrey[4]
Ben Davis Junior High School
MSD Wayne Township
Indianapolis, IN

Concepts: ***Need to <u>Know</u> About <u>Polynomials</u>***
Indiana Standard 6

Polynomial Terms
- Monomial
- Binomial
- Trinomial
- Quadratic
- Powers
- Roots/solutions

Factoring Polynomials
- Common monomial factors
- Difference of two perfect squares
- Factors of other quadratics

Solving Polynomials
- Solution of an equation
- Zeroes of function
- x-intercepts

Skills: ***Be Able to <u>Do</u>***

- Add, subtract, multiply, divide (polynomials)
- Find (powers, roots, common factors)
- Factor (polynomials)
- Understand and describe (solutions of polynomials)

Topics or Context:

- Graphing calculator
- Polynomial unit
- Real-life story problems

Big Ideas

1. Polynomial and quadratic expressions model real life.

2. You can use factoring to efficiently solve certain quadratic equations.

3. Equations generate various lines, curves, and shapes.

Essential Questions

1. What are quadratics and polynomials? Where and when do you use them?

2. How can quadratic equations be solved?

3. What different types of graphs can be predicted from equations?

---

[4] Reprinted with permission.

EARTH SCIENCE
Grade 6
Maria Guerrero, Pamela Ortiz, Salvador Martin, Marina Wallis, and Kim Woods[5]
Lennox Middle School
Lennox, California

Concepts: ***Need to <u>Know</u> About <u>Plate Tectonics</u>***

Layers of the Earth

Plate Movement

Earthquakes
- Faults
- Fissures
- San Andreas
- Epicenter
- Effects

Volcanoes
- Layers
- Mono Lake

Mid-Ocean Ridges
- Layers

Mountain Buildings
- Rock Cycle
- Fossils
- Climatic Zones
- San Gabriel/Sierras

Skills: ***Be Able to <u>Do</u>***
- Compare and Contrast
- Identify
- Label
- Observe
- Differentiate
- Predict
- Locate
- Synthesize
- Analyze
- Cause and Effect

[5] Reprinted with permission.

(continued)

Grade 6, **Maria Guerrero, Pamela Ortiz, Salvador Martin, Marina Wallis, and Kim Woods,**
Lennox Middle School, Lennox, California *(continued)*

Topics or Context:

- Earthquakes
- Volcanoes
- Climatic zones
- Natural disasters
- Mid-ocean ridges
- Fossils
- Rock cycle
- Trenches
- Subduction zones
- Lithosphere
- Core, crust, mantle

Big Ideas

1. The earth's surface continues to change.

2. Volcanism, earthquakes, and mountain building are interrelated.

3. Earthquakes, volcanic eruptions, and mountain building are the result of plate tectonics.

4. Plate movement is in response to heat convection within the mantle.

Essential Questions

1. How has the earth's surface changed over time, and how do you predict it will change in the future?

2. How are volcanism, earthquakes, and mountain building interrelated?

3. What evidence is there that shows/proves that plate tectonics exist?

4. How does heat energy within the earth affect plate movement?

**Maria Guerrero, Pamela Ortiz, Salvador Martin,
Marina Wallis, and Kim Woods**[6]
Lennox Middle School
Lennox, California

Concepts: ***Need to <u>Know</u> About <u>Heat Energy</u>***
California Standard #3

Energy
- Transports
  - Through solids by conduction
  - Through liquids by conduction or convection
  - By heat flow, waves, and moving objects

Heat energy released affects weather
- Solar
  - Transferred by radiation
  - Powers wind, ocean currents, and the water cycle
  - Balances

Skills: ***Be Able to <u>Do</u>***

- Compare and contrast
- Identify
- Label
- Observe
- Differentiate
- Predict
- Locate
- Analyze
- Cause and effect

Topics or Context:

- Transportation
- Heat
- Waves
- Conduction
- Convection
- Radiation
- Potential and Kinetic Energy
- Solar Energy
- Pressure
- Air Movement
- Humidity
- Weather
- Winds
- Ocean Currents
- Water Cycle

[6] Reprinted with permission.

(continued)

SCIENCE

Grade 6, **Maria Guerrero, Pamela Ortiz, Salvador Martin, Marina Wallis, and Kim Woods,**
Lennox Middle School, Lennox, California *(continued)*

Big Ideas

1. Heat constantly moves from warmer objects to cooler objects until all the objects are at the same temperature.

2. When fuel is consumed, most of the energy released becomes heat energy.

3. Everything has heat energy.

4. The state of matter of an object will determine how the heat is transferred.

5. Heat energy affects weather.

Essential Questions

1. How does heat seek to balance the temperature of objects?

2. What happens when fuel is consumed?

3. How is energy released?

4. How can you find the heat energy of any object?

5. How is heat transferred from object to object?

6. How are heat energy and weather related?

LIFE SCIENCE
Grade 7
Vicki Jarnett, Joel McKinney, and John Mutz[7]
South Wayne Junior High
MSD Wayne Township
Indianapolis, Indiana

Concepts: ***Need to <u>Know</u> About <u>The Living Environment</u>***

Diversity and Interdependence of Life
- Comparative anatomy
  - External
  - Internal
  - Taxonomy
- Cells
  - Structure
  - Function
- Food webs
  - Ocean
  - Land
  - Photosynthesis
- Reproduction
- Populations and environmental factors
  - Habitats
  - Predator/prey
  - Food depletion

Human Identity—Impacts on Human Population
- Technologies
  - Food production
  - Sanitation
  - Disease prevention
- Lifestyles
  - Nutrition
  - Exercise
- Organisms
  - Viruses
  - Bacteria
  - Fungi
  - Parasites
- Immune systems
  - White blood cells
  - Antibodies
- Pollution
  - Air
  - Water
  - Soil

[7] Reprinted with permission.

(continued)

Skills: **Be Able to <u>Do</u>**

- Recognize (similarities, differences, interactions, cause and effect)
- Understand (similarities, differences, interactions, interdependencies)
- Observe (characteristics, structures)
- Examine (structures, functions)
- Describe (technologies, similarities, differences, processes)
- Explain (processes, functions, structures, cause and effect)
- Trace (interactions)
- Distinguish (organisms)
- Classify (organisms, structures)
- Infer (relationships)
- Use (instruments, technologies)

Topics or Context:

- Cell Unit
- Environmental Study
- Comparative Anatomy Unit
- Human Population Unit

Big Ideas

1. Life forms share many commonalities due to their degree of relatedness.

2. All living matter and energy flow through the ecosystems.

3. Technology, lifestyles, other organisms, pollution, and natural defenses impact the human population.

Essential Questions

1. What are some common things that all life forms share? Why is this so?

2. How do organisms interact to transfer matter and energy?

3. What forces and conditions impact human life? How?

LIFE SCIENCE
Grade 7
Nellie Rios-Parra, Angela Fajardo, Aileen Martin, and Sal Gumina[8]
Lennox Middle School
Lennox, California

Concepts: ***Need to <u>Know</u> About <u>Genetics</u>***

- Cell structure: DNA location
- Sexual and asexual organisms in terms of life cycle and reproduction
- Reproduction
- Inherited traits
    - Dominant
    - Recessive

Skills: ***Be Able to <u>Do</u>***

- Distinguish (compare and contrast) difference between sexual and asexual organism

Topics or Context:

- DNA
- Sexual and asexual organisms
- Reproduction
- Traits and genes

Big Ideas

1. Traits and dynamics and can be influenced and modified by the environment.

2. Cells or organisms typically contain genetic instructions that specify its traits.

Essential Question

1. How does the environment affect the manifestation of certain traits?

[8] Reprinted with permission.

PHYSICAL SCIENCE
Grade 8
Marlene Wilson, Larry Lamadrid, Elisa Glass, and Ellen Ipson[9]
Lennox Middle School
Lennox, California

Concepts: ***Need to <u>Know</u> About <u>Energy Forces</u>***
California Science Standard #2

- Force has direction and magnitude
- Cumulative effect of forces
- Net forces determine the motion and velocity of an object
- Different forces that act upon a static object
- Relationship of mass and force
- Role of gravity

Skills: ***Be Able to <u>Do</u>***

- Measure
- Calculate
- Identify
- Interpret
- Predict
- Compare and contrast
- Observe

Topics or Context:

- Newton's laws of motion
- Simple machines as a means to teaching force
- Force as it relates to work

Big Idea

1. Unbalanced forces cause changes in velocity.

Essential Questions

1. What are the three laws of motion?

2. How is work related to force?

3. How does friction work?

4. How do you apply these laws to real-life situations?

---

[9] Reprinted with permission.

PHYSICAL SCIENCE
Grade 8
Marlene Wilson, Larry Lamadrid, Elisa Glass, and Ellen Ipson[10]
Lennox Middle School
Lennox, California

Concepts: ***Need to <u>Know</u> About <u>Chemistry</u>***

- Carbon has the central role in the chemistry of living organisms
- Living organisms are composed of carbon, hydrogen, nitrogen, phosphorus, oxygen, and sulfur
- These six elements make up most of the Earth's biomass
- Living organisms are composed of many different sizes of molecules

Skills: ***Be Able to <u>Do</u>***

- Identify
- Describe
- Define
- Connect
- Combine
- Model

Topics or Context:

- Carbon chemistry
- Food chemistry

The Big Idea

1. Chemistry underlies the functioning of biological systems.

Essential Questions

1. How and why does carbon play an essential role in living organisms?

2. How does the composition of different molecules contribute to their function in the body?

---

[10] Reprinted with permission.

LIFE SCIENCE
Grade 8
Author

Concepts: ***Need to <u>Know</u> About <u>The Living Environment</u>***
Indiana Science Standard 4

Diversity of Life
- Inherited traits
- Acquired skills
- Organisms w/genes from single parents
- Organisms w/sexes, genes from both parents
- Selective breeding
  – Cultivated plants
  – Domestic animals

Life and Evolution
- Ecosystem
- Interdependence
- Matter transfer
  – One organism to another
  – Organism to environment
- Energy—origin and transfer
- How animals get and release energy
- Impact of environment on individual

Human Identity
- Fossil evidence
- Human evolution

Skills: ***Be Able to <u>Do</u>***
(Ideally, Verb Targets should be added from standards text for greater clarity)

- Trace
- Understand
- Differentiate (compare and contrast)
- Describe
- Recognize
- Explain

Topics or Context:

- Life Science Unit

(continued)

Big Ideas

1. Life forms reflect inherited traits, genetically cultivated traits, and acquired skills.

2. All living matter and energy flow through ecosystems.

3. Environment impacts the way people live.

4. Human evolution can be traced through fossil evidence.

Essential Questions

1. Why do life forms behave the way they do? How do acquired skills and inherited or genetically altered traits impact all forms of matter?

2. Where does energy come from? How is it transferred between life forms?

3. What role does the environment play on individuals and their life experiences?

4. How does science explain the evolution of human beings?

Grade 7
David Done and Cheri Sterling[11]
Gilbert High School (West and South)
Anaheim Union High School District
Anaheim, California

Concepts:	***Need to <u>Know</u> About the <u>Roman Empire</u>***

1. Geography and expansion
    a. Strengths
    b. Contributions
        i.   Citizenship
        ii.   Rights
        iii. Art
        iv.   Architecture
        v.   Engineering
        vi.   Philosophy
        vii. Christianity
    c. Decline/weaknesses
        i.   internal power struggles
        ii.   corruption
        iii. undermining of citizenship
        iv.   education and lack of news
        v.   economic
    d. East-West split
        i.   religion
        ii.   culture

Skills: ***Be Able to <u>Do</u>***

*   Show (understanding)
*   Recognize (cause and effect)
*   Understand (historical events)

Topics or Context:

*   Roman Empire Unit

---

[11] Reprinted with permission.

(continued)

Big Ideas

1. Power corrupts.

2. Expansion carries consequences.

3. Technology enhances economic development.

4. Political exclusion leads to unrest.

5. Religion affects society.

Essential Questions

1. What were the consequences of Roman expansion?

2. How did the Roman political system become corrupt?

3. What factors led to Roman economic expansion?

4. How did religion affect the Roman Empire?

5. How was the growth of the Roman Empire similar to that of the US? How was it different?

6. What lessons can we learn from the decline of the Roman Empire?

WORLD HISTORY (Medieval Africa)
Grade 7
Grant Schuster, James Urquidez, and Chris Esperanza[12]
Dale & Sycamore Junior High Schools
Anaheim Union High School District
Anaheim, California

Concepts: ***Need to <u>Know</u> About <u>Medieval Africa</u>***

Geography
- Niger River
- Vegetation zones
  - Semi-arid
  - Tropical rain forest
  - Savannah
  - Desert

Politics
- Ghana and Mali empires
- Influence of Islamic beliefs, ethics, and laws on native cultures

Economics
- Regional commerce
- Trans-Saharan caravan trade
- Gold and salt trade
- Slave trade

Religions
- Native religions
- Islam
- Interaction between native and Islamic cultures (Koumbi)

Social Structures
- Labor specialization
- Family (kinship)
- Written and oral traditions

Skills: ***Be Able to <u>Do</u>***

Study
- Relationship of vegetation zones to lifestyles of inhabitants
- Trade and development of Ghana and Mali empires

Analyze
- Importance of family, labor specialization, commerce
- Values, ethics, and laws of natives and Muslims

[12] Reprinted with permission.   *(continued)*

Describe
- Role of trans-Saharan trade in changing religion and culture
- Importance of written and oral traditions in the transmission of African history and culture

Evaluate
- Complex relations of natives with Muslims

Topics or Context:

- Medieval West Africa

Big Ideas

1. Environment dictates lifestyle.

2. Values and culture are passed from generation to generation.

3. Converging societies experience both conflict and progress.

4. Growth in commerce creates wealth in empires.

5. Availability and need determine value of resources.

Essential Questions

1. What were the different environments of West Africa? How did each affect the lifestyle of people who lived there?

2. What methods did West Africa use to pass on values and culture? What was its purpose in doing so?

3. How did the blending of Muslim and Native African cultures create progress and conflict in Africa?

4. What role did the trans-Saharan trade routes play in the development of West African empires?

5. What were the most valued resources in West Africa? Why were they so valuable?

U.S. HISTORY
Grade 8
Joni McGinnis and Jeff Hayes[13]
Tracy Unified School District
Tracy, California

Concepts: ***Need to <u>Know</u> About <u>U.S. Constitution</u>***

CONCEPTS	SKILLS
Historical Documents: Magna Carta, Mayflower Compact, English Bill of Rights, Declaration of Independence, Articles of Confederation, Constitution, Federalist Papers, and the Statute for Religious Freedoms.	Understand Describe Discuss
Founding Fathers: Madison, Hamilton, Jay, Washington, Sherman, Morris, Wilson, Jefferson.	Compare
American Principles of Democracy: • Indian policies • Separation of church and state • Idea of constitutionalism • Preserve individual rights	Analyze Evaluate

Big Idea

1. Early documents and leaders shaped American policy and brought about national and individual security.

Essential Questions

1. How have opposing views of the forefathers shaped American policy?

2. How did the blending of important documents lead to the formation of the Constitution?

3. How does the Constitution promote individual and national security?

4. Is the Constitution relevant to American citizens today? Why or why not?

---

[13] Reprinted with permission.

VISUAL ARTS — Design and Production
Jane Domach and Dennis Pociask[14]
Horning Middle School
Whittier Elementary
Waukesha, Wisconsin

Concepts: ***Need to <u>Know</u> About <u>Art Ideas and the</u>
<u>Creative Process</u>***
Wisconsin Standards C1 through C9

- Elements and principles of design
- Sketches
- Techniques
- Characteristics of materials
- Craftsmanship
- Quality design
- Meaning
- "Show Worthy"

Skills: ***Be Able to <u>Do</u>***

- Know (elements and principles of design; meaning)
- Understand (quality design; characteristics of materials)
- Use (design techniques, sketches)
- Develop (craftsmanship, ideas, and originality)
- Reflect (one's creative process)

Topics or Context:

- Variety of art projects using different media

Big Ideas

1. The meaning of an artwork can be affected by its design.

2. Different art materials enable the artist to create a variety of effects or results.

3. The thought process is ongoing in the creation of art.

4. Art involves finding solutions to problems.

Essential Questions

1. Why do different art works use different styles?

2. Why do artists use different materials?

3. Why do artists change their ideas as they work?

4. Why do people create art?

---

[14] Reprinted with permission.

BUSINESS EDUCATION
Grade 8
Janet Merten and Julie Richter[15]
Horning Middle School
School District of Waukesha
Waukesha, Wisconsin

Standard: Students will explore careers and develop skills to make meaningful decisions for his/her future.

Indicators: K.8.1–K.8.11, K8.13

Concepts: **Need to _Know_ About _CAREER PLANNING_**

Personal Traits
- Talents and interests
- Strengths/weaknesses (self and career)
- Self-management skills
- Work values

Exploring Careers
- Skills and aptitudes
- Career options
- Education options
- Resources (counselors, Holland codes, video series, WCIS-Career Visions, Internet)
- Global opportunities
- Job application

Career Portfolio
- Tentative Education Plan (TEP)
- Career Information Sheet
- Resume
- Self-Directed Search
- Holland Themes
- Career Searches (2)
- About ME Sheet
- Career Match Printout
- Optional: Internship Interest Form, Job Shadow Evaluation

Skills: **Be Able to _Do_**

Identify (talents, interests, strengths and weaknesses, aptitudes, career and education options, global opportunities)

Use (resources, strengths and weaknesses)

Demonstrate/Apply (mock interviews, etiquette, job application skills)

---

[15] Reprinted with permission.

(continued)

Develop	(job interview skills, career portfolio)
Transfer	(knowledge and skills through Junior Achievement, job shadowing, and real-world experiences)
Create	(resumes, ME bag)

Topics or Context:

- Self-assessment tools
- Self-directed searches/Holland codes
- Career counselor
- Career searches using career visions and other resources
- Career summary activity
- Career profile (about ME)
- Job shadowing experiences
- Job application
- Resume
- Mock interview
- Career portfolio
- ME bag

Big Ideas

1. Skills we learn in class will be used in the real world.

2. Skill, strength, and weakness assessments will help us identify future careers.

3. Resources we use in class can help us to locate career information in our future.

4. Items we place in our career portfolio can be used to find, be hired for, and keep jobs in our future.

Essential Questions

1. Why do we need to learn certain skills?

2. Why should we assess our own skills, strengths, and weaknesses as we consider finding employment?

3. What resources do we need in order to find career information?

4. What items/documents should be included in a career portfolio?

BUSINESS EDUCATION
Grade 8
Evelyn G. Scharlau[16]
Butler Middle School
School District of Waukesha
Waukesha, Wisconsin

Concepts:

Need to <u>Know</u> About <u>Formatting and Writing Business Letters and Designing Stationery</u>

Wisconsin English/Language Arts Standard: B.8.1

Wisconsin Academic Standards for Business Education: A.8.1, B.8.6, B.8.9, B.8.10

Writing
- Business letter correspondence: formatting and composing
- Expository business letter
- Edit and revise

Technology
- Computer
- Word-processing software
- Printer

Skills:

Be Able to <u>Do</u>

- Revise (personalize information in teacher-prepared business letters)
- Compose (missing information and information to be personalized in two business letters, write one complete business letter)
- Demonstrate (correct grammar, mechanics, word usage)
- Use variety of technologies (word-processing software, pen and pencil)
- Proofread and edit (business letters, designed stationery, envelope address and format)
- Produce (one handwritten business letter, two keyboarded business letters, envelope on computer, designed stationery and envelope)

Topics or Context:

Skills
- Business letter format
- Envelope format
- Word-processing software

[16] Reprinted with permission.

(continued)

Grade 8, **Evelyn G. Scharlau,** Butler Middle School, School District of Waukesha, Waukesha, Wisconsin *(continued)*

Production:
- One handwritten business letter
- Two keyboarded business letters
- Handmade stationery and envelope
- Computer stationery
- Computer envelope

Big Ideas

1. When composing business letters, use the correct letter parts and organize and format the parts correctly.

2. Use of correct grammar, mechanics, and word usage in business letters creates a good impression.

3. Editing and revising are necessary when composing all business letter parts so that all text is accurate.

4. Word-processing skills are essential to produce professional-looking business letters.

Essential Questions

1. What parts are used when composing a business letter? How are the parts of a letter organized?

2. Why are correct grammar, mechanics, and word usage essential in business letters?

3. Why are editing and revising necessary when writing business letters?

4. Why are computer skills necessary when composing and formatting business letters? Which skills are needed?

PERFORMING ARTS — Music (Orchestra, Choir, and Band)
Grades 6 – 8
Randy McMillan[17]
Monte Vista Middle School
Tracy Unified School District
Tracy, California

Concepts: ***Need to <u>Know</u> About <u>Reading and Notating Music</u>***
California Music Standards 1.1, 1.2, 1.3, 2.4

Read, Notate, and Perform Music
- Intervals
- Triads
- Rhythmic Notation
- Melodic Notation

Standard Symbols
- Pitch
- Meter
- Rhythm
- Dynamics
- Tempo (double and triple)

Composition
- Simple Rhythmic Compositions

Skills: ***Be Able to <u>Do</u>***

- Read (notation, intervals, triads)
- Write (notation, intervals, triads)
- Perform (voice or instrument)
- Transcribe (rhythmic notation)
- Compose (simple melodies/rhythms)

Topics or Context:

- Theory Unit
- Rhythm Activity (Reading and Performing)
- Worksheets
- Rhythm Transcribing
- Vocabulary Test
- Composing Original Rhythmic Music

[17] Reprinted with permission.   *(continued)*

Big Ideas

1. Understanding how music is written will help you understand what the composer wants, and perform it better.

2. Standard symbols tell you how to play or sing written music.

3. Composing your own music will help you better understand and appreciate music written by others.

Essential Questions

1. Why do you need to read written music?

2. How do we know what to play or sing when performing written music?

3. Why practice writing your own music?

PHYSICAL EDUCATION
Grade 8
Melissa Hendricks and Marjorie Sims[18]
Metropolitan School District of Wayne Township
Indianapolis, Indiana

Concepts:	***Need to <u>Know</u> About <u>Team Sports</u>***

Indiana Physical Education Standards 1, 5, 6, 7

Motor Skills
- Fundamental techniques (8.1.1)
- Movement patterns (8.1.2)

Rules
- Safety (8.5.2)
- Sportsmanship (8.6.4)

Teamwork
- Social interaction (8.7.3)
- Leadership skills (8.5.1)
- Recognizing differences and abilities (8.6.3)

Skills:	***Be Able to <u>Do</u>***

- Apply
- Demonstrate
- Refine

Topics or Context:

- Demonstrations
- Lead-up game
- Skill practice

Big Ideas

1. Teamwork promotes cooperation and a positive interaction among individuals.
2. Skill development enhances motivation, self-esteem, and physical growth.
3. Rules of conduct and game rules are necessary for fair play in life.
4. Respect should be given to all students regardless of personal differences or skill levels.

Essential Questions

1. Why is teamwork a necessary life skill?
2. How does skill development relate to increased motivation, self-esteem, and physical growth?
3. How do game rules relate to rules of daily living?
4. How does understanding personal differences in sport activities compare to understanding individual differences in your daily lives?

[18] Reprinted with permission.

PHYSICAL EDUCATION: FITNESS
(Also Applicable to High School)
Gary Moore, Jolene Azevedo, Chelsea Stephens, and Chuck Selna[19]
Tracy Unified School District
Tracy, California

Concepts:

Need to <u>Know</u> About <u>Fitness</u>
District P.E. Standard(s): 2.1.1, 2.1.2, 2.1.3

Positive Self-Image:
- Self-Esteem
- Self-Respect
- Confidence
- Body Composition

Individual Fitness Program
- Target Heart Rate
- Aerobic/Anaerobic Exercise
- Stretching
- Stress Level
- Weight Training
- Time and Frequency
- Personal Goals
- Sports Interests

Skills:

Be Able to <u>Do</u>

- Demonstrate (skills to reduce stress)
- Demonstrate (problem-solving skills in group setting)
- Demonstrate (cooperation, acceptance, and belonging within a group or team activity)
- Understand (Heart Rate Zone)
- Find (Target Heart Rate)
- Understand (difference between aerobic and anaerobic activity)
- Compose (obtainable goals for personal and physical fitness)
- Identify (sports-specific muscle groups)
- Recognize (general concepts of sports)

Topics or Context:

- Fitness unit
- Team cooperation unit
- Individual sports unit
- Team sports unit

---

[19] Reprinted with permission.

(continued)

Big Ideas

1. No matter the amount of stress in your environment, always strive to obtain the best for yourself.

2. Show respect for all students regardless of personal differences or fitness levels so cultural and physical barriers break down.

3. It is necessary to participate in physical activity to maintain a healthy lifestyle.

4. Working out properly guarantees that maximum potential and benefits are met.

Essential Questions

1. What are some things that affect the way we feel about ourselves? How do we overcome them?

2. What does respect look like?

3. Why should you be physically active?

4. What does working out mean to you? How does it help you?

CHAPTER EIGHT

High School Standards "Unwrapped"

In this chapter dedicated to the high school grades, 9 through 12, I have included numerous examples of "unwrapped" standards and indicators from several content areas, particularly language arts, mathematics, science, and social studies. You may also wish to review the middle school examples in the previous chapter. Several of these may be adaptable to high school grades.

These "unwrapped" examples were created by me and by seminar participants in different states. I have received permission from these educators to reprint their work for the publication of this book. A few of the examples included were submitted anonymously during the guided practice "unwrapping" activity at the seminar.

Please note: I have not included the full text of the standards and indicators along with the graphic organizer of "unwrapped" concepts and skills. Although inclusion of the full text would indeed have been helpful, particularly for educators in the individual states from which the "unwrapped" standards originate, printing limitations made this infeasible. Certain examples do identify particular states and standards, however.

Lastly, a few of the graphic organizers do not include parenthetical "targets" after the skills. The educators involved either chose not to include them, or they attended one of my earlier "unwrapping" standards seminars where I did not emphasize their importance to the degree that I do now.

The central purpose for including these examples is to provide readers with a wide variety of graphic organizers, Big Ideas, and Essential Questions in several content areas that they can reference to more fully comprehend the "unwrapping" process. To all those who have generously contributed to this collection of examples, I thank you on behalf of all educators whose understanding of how to "unwrap" will deepen as a result of your work.

LANGUAGE ARTS — Integrated Reading and Writing
Grade 9
Melissa Coons and Julie Volbers[1]
Ben Davis Junior High School
MSD Wayne Township
Indianapolis, Indiana

Concepts: ***Need to Know About Grade 9 READING***

General Concepts

1. Literal Word Meanings
2. Implied Word Meanings
3. Paraphrasing of Ideas
4. Comparison of Literary Works to Real-Life Situations

Recognition of Different Forms of Literature

1. Comedy
2. Tragedy
3. Dramatic Monologue
4. Fiction
5. Nonfiction
6. Biographical/Autobiographical

Skills: ***Be Able to Do***

1. Distinguish (word meanings)
2. Interpret (implied word meanings)
3. Synthesize (content)
4. Paraphrase (ideas)
5. Connect (to related topics)
6. Demonstrate (comprehension)
7. Explain (connection to reality)

Topics or Context:

1. Novels
2. Short Stories
3. Performance Assessments
4. Poetry
5. Other Literary Works

---

[1] Reprinted with permission.   *(continued)*

Concepts: ***Need to <u>Know</u> About <u>Grade 9 WRITING</u>***

Emotional Appeal

1. Organization of Ideas

Rhetorical Communication

1. Personal Anecdote
2. Case Study
3. Analogy

Defending Positions

1. Evidence
2. Facts
3. Expert Opinions
4. Beliefs
5. Logical Reasoning
6. Quotations

General Concepts

1. Thesis Development
2. Tone and Focus
3. Accurate Spelling
4. Correct Use of Punctuation
5. Correct Use of Spelling

Skills: ***Be Able to <u>Do</u>***

1. Establish (thesis)
2. Convey (perspective)
3. Maintain (tone and focus)
4. Write
5. Organize
6. Clarify
7. Defend (position)
8. Address (issues)
9. Produce (legible work)
10. Demonstrate (comprehension)

(continued)

Big Ideas for Teachers

1. A variety of literature pieces reveal themes involving controversial, emotional, and realistic issues.

2. Emotional appeal and rhetorical communication enhance persuasive writing and help people relate to relevant experiences.

3. Cohesive thesis development enhances the meaning for the audience.

4. Speech delivery involves clarification of the author's purpose while the listener distinguishes the author's point of view and gains understanding through reflection.

Big Ideas for Students

1. Literature provokes emotion through controversial and realistic issues.

2. Literature and writing force (compel) us to defend our beliefs using real-life experiences.

3. The main idea of the writing is stated in the thesis statement.

Essential Questions

1. How does a literary work reveal underlying themes common to all humans?

2. How does the author's use of words challenge your beliefs?

3. What are the main ideas presented in the author's work? (How does an author convey his message to the reader?) How do these main ideas relate to other cultural experiences?

LANGUAGE ARTS
Grade 9
Anonymous

Concepts: ***Need to <u>Know</u> About <u>Research</u> Skills***

- Accessing resources
- Plagiarism
- Citations
  - MLA
  - APA
- Point of view
- Distinguishing between credible and unreliable resources

Skills: ***Be Able to <u>Do</u>***

- Narrow (topic)
- Formulate (hypothesis)
- Locate (resources)
- Take (notes)
  - Paraphrase
  - Quote directly
  - Organize
- Cite (sources)
- Synthesize/comprehend (research)
- Writing process skills
  - Draft
  - Revise
  - Edit

Topics or Context:

- Research paper related to current unit

Big Ideas

1. Research is a multi-step process that begins with a specific idea and results in a fact-based product.

2. Research requires citation of sources in an ethical manner.

3. Consumer products have all been developed through research.

Essential Questions

1. What is research? What does it enable us to produce?

2. How can you use others' work in your own?

3. How is research relevant to daily life?

LANGUAGE ARTS
Grade 10
Anonymous

Concepts: ***Need to <u>Know</u> About <u>Persuasive Writing</u>***

Prewriting
- Strategies
- Thesis
  - Clear position
  - Perspective

Research
- Clear methods
- Supportive evidence
- Synthesis from multiple resources

Writing
- Organized paragraphs
- Structure
  - Major points and evidence
  - Reader concerns and counterevidence
- Transitions

Revising
- Organization
  - Controlling
- Word choice
- Technology

Skills: ***Organized by Steps in Writing Process***

Prewrite
- Brainstorm
- Outline
- Establish (thesis)
- Create (structure and transitions)
- Reorganize (notes)

Write
- State (thesis)
- Support (points)
- Employ (evidence)
- Anticipate and Address (concerns)
- Create (balance)

(continued)

Revise
- Improve (word choice, logic)
- Edit
  - Tone for audience
  - Spelling
  - Punctuation
  - Grammar

Topics or Context:

- Argumentative essay
- Opinion papers
- Pro/Con
- Research paper

Big Ideas

1. Writing is a systematic process that demands multiple revisions.

2. Research brings together divergent viewpoints.

3. Personal opinions gain strength when supported by facts and reasons.

4. Writers communicate in different forms for different purposes and audiences.

Essential Questions

1. How do we know when our writing is finished?

2. Why do writers research?

3. How are we influenced by what others write?

4. Why do writers learn different formats for expressing their ideas?

LANGUAGE ARTS
Grade 10
Amanda Ammer and Anne Koenig[2]
Oakwood High School
Oakwood, Ohio

Concepts: **Need to <u>Know</u> About <u>Writing Applications</u>**

Narratives
- Story with beginning, middle, end
- Characterizations through actions, words, feelings
- Setting with details
- Figurative language

Responses to Literature
- Awareness of author's style
- Interpretation of literary work's significance
- Effects of work on audience

Informational Essays
- Thesis statement
- Supporting details
- Effective introduction and conclusion
- Organizational patterns

Research-Based Reports
- Source citations

Persuasive Essays
- Logical argument
- Supporting evidence

Functional Documents
- Request for information
- Resume
- Letters of complaint
- Thank-you note
- Invitations
- Friendly letter
- Business letter
- Envelope

Informal Writings
- Daily journaling

[2] Reprinted with permission.

(continued)

Grade 10, Amanda Ammer and Anne Koenig, Oakwood High School,
Oakwood, Ohio *(continued)*

Skills: ***Be Able to <u>Do</u>***

- Identify (parts of a letter, envelope)
- Relate (a coherent storyline)
- Develop (characters, setting, details, awareness of style and audience, thesis)
- Generate (citations, arguments)
- Support (ideas, evidence)
- Organize (thesis, details, intro, conclusion, structure)
- Write (figurative language, interpretation of literature, functional documents, journals, informational essays, persuasive essays)

Topics or Context:

- Responses to curricular prompts
- Safety
- Daily living
- Employment

Big Ideas

1. Clear writing is critical to accurate communication.

2. Different types of writing contain different elements.

3. Writing enhances learning.

Essential Questions

1. Why it is important to write clearly?

2. Do we always write the same way? Why do we write?

3. How can writing help us?

SPEECH
Grade 11
MaryAnn Krause and Stephanie Gilmore[3]
Waukesha North
Waukesha Public Schools
Waukesha, Wisconsin

Concepts: ***Need to <u>Know</u> About <u>Persuasive Speaking</u>***

Reading: A12.1, A12.4
Oral Language: C12.1, 12.2, 12.3
Research and Inquiry: F12.1

Research
- Research Strategies
- Authoritative Sources

Organization
- Deductive/Inductive Reasoning
- Propaganda Techniques

Delivery
- Effective Verbal and Nonverbal Speaking Strategies

Evaluation
- Faulty Reasoning

Skills: ***Be Able to <u>Do</u>***

Research
- Distinguish (fact from opinion)
- Evaluate (reliability of data and sources)
- Summarize (main ideas)

Organization
- Construct (a coherent argument)
- Apply (tests of logic and reasoning)
- Synthesize and Integrate (data)
- Cite (sources)

Delivery
- Demonstrate (confidence and poise)

Evaluation
- Analyze (messages for accuracy)

[3] Reprinted with permission.

(continued)

Grade 11, **MaryAnn Krause and Stephanie Gilmore,** Waukesha North,
Waukesha Public Schools, Waukesha, Wisconsin *(continued)*

Big Ideas

1. Opinion merely expresses a person's point of view; persuasion convinces others to share in that same viewpoint.

2. Persuasion needs to be backed by evidence and reasoning.

3. Persuasion needs to be well-organized and documented.

4. Effective persuasion can achieve your goals.

5. Effective persuasion can be beneficial as well as destructive.

Essential Questions

1. Do opinion and persuasion mean the same thing?

2. What enhances persuasion?

3. What is the benefit of being able to persuade your listeners?

4. How can persuasion be both good and bad?

LITERARY CRITICISM
Grade 11
Gary Moorman, Stephanie Nixon, and Christie Sinclair[4]
Ben Davis High School
MSD Wayne Township
Indianapolis, IN

Concepts: ***Need to <u>Know</u> About <u>Literary Criticism</u>***

Indiana Reading Standard 3

Political assumptions on a variety of topics
- Clarity
- Consistency

Literary works/Essays
- Philosophical arguments
- Authors' positions
- Credibility of characters

Skills: ***Be Able to <u>Do</u>***

- Analyze
  - Political assumptions
  - Philosophical arguments
  - Quality of works

Topics or Context:

- Politically significant works of American literature
- Novels contain philosophical arguments of American writers

Big Ideas

1. Political and philosophical arguments are key components of American literature.

2. The author's position is revealed through the characters in the literary work.

3. How an author conveys his or her individual position contributes to the quality of work.

Essential Questions

1. What arguments can be found throughout American literature?

2. How does the reader determine the author's position?

3. How can the reader determine the quality of literary work?

---

[4] Reprinted with permission.

SHAKESPEARE
Grade 12
Patricia Drake, Maria McFarland, and Ellen Isbell[5]
Centerville High School
Centerville, Ohio

Concepts:

Need to <u>Know</u> About <u>Literary Understanding</u> <u>of Shakespeare</u>

Structural Elements of Fiction
- Plot
- Theme
- Character
- Mood
- Setting

Literary Understanding
- New vocabulary
- Comprehension techniques
- Unfamiliar terms
- Author's development of literary concepts

Dramatic Elements
- Dramatic irony
- Soliloquy
- Monologue
- Asides
- Tragic flaw
- Tragic hero
- Comic relief
- Stage directions

Skills:

Be Able to <u>Do</u>

- Discuss
- Recognize
- Compare/contrast
- Question
- Summarize
- Evaluate
- Predict
- Interpret
- Analyze

Topics or Context:

- Hamlet
- Othello

[5] Reprinted with permission.

(continued)

Big Ideas

1. The themes of betrayal and revenge are found in daily life.

2. Change impacts family dynamics.

3. Culture and history are reflected in literature.

4. Differentiating between fact and fiction is necessary to get to the truth.

5. Dramatic elements bring literature to life.

Essential Questions

1. Why are the works of Shakespeare still so contemporary?

2. What does the study of the past teach us?

3. Why can the truth be so difficult to know?

4. Why does "timeless" literature require literary devices?

ALGEBRA II

Sherry Gramer, Gary Mahoney, Ross McKenna, and Mike Davidson[6]
Ben Davis High School
MSD Wayne Township
Indianapolis, IN

Concepts: ***Need to <u>Know</u> About <u>Sequences and Series</u>***
Algebra II Indiana Standard 8

Sequences
- Arithmetic
  - Common difference
  - Specified term
- Geometric
  - Common difference
  - Specified term

Series
- Sigma notation
- Arithmetic
- Geometric
- Infinite
- Partial sum

Skills: ***Be Able to <u>Do</u>***
- Define (sequence/series)
- Manipulate (formulas for specific variable)
- Compute (terms, sums)
- Select (appropriate formula)
- Apply (to real life)

Topics or Context:
- Textbook chapter on sequence and series

Big Ideas

1. Mathematical sequences and series are essential tools for problem solving.
2. Formulas can be manipulated to find a specific term.
3. Mathematical sequences and series can be applied to real-life situations.

Essential Questions

1. What are mathematical sequences and series?
2. What are the formulas for arithmetic and geometric sequences and series? How do you use them?
3. Why are sequence and series formulas important to learn?

[6] Reprinted with permission.

ALGEBRA — Collaboratively with Chemistry, Computer Information Systems, and Nursing
Grades 10–12
Mary E. Brown (Computer Information Systems), Wesley Clark (Chemistry), and Barbara Ellington (Practical Nursing)[7]
Norfolk Technical Vocational Center
Norfolk, Virginia

Concepts: **Need to _Know_ About _Organizing, Manipulating, and Analyzing Data_**
Related Virginia Standards of Learning

Matrices
- Addition
- Subtraction
- Scalar Multiplication

Patterns
- Algebraic
- Graphic

Relationships
- Function

Skills: **Be Able to _Do_**
- Organize
- Manipulate
- Analyze
- Represent (pattern)
- Determine (if a function)

Topics or Context:

- Data Sources — Situations in
  - Business
  - Science
  - Industry
  - Consumer

Big Ideas

1. Organizing and manipulating data are important in the analysis process.
2. Analysis helps determine if a pattern exists.
3. Patterns help to determine if a relationship is a function.
4. If there is a solution, you can find it.

Essential Questions

1. Why is it important to organize data?
2. Why do we analyze anyway?
3. Why look for patterns?
4. Is there a solution to every problem?

[7] Reprinted with permission.

ALGEBRA
Grade 12
Suzanne Husman, Steve Hatch, and Jim Truszynski[8]
Waukesha, Wisconsin

Concepts: **Need to <u>Know</u> About <u>Algebraic Relationships</u>**
Wisconsin Standards F 12.1 through F 12.4

Patterns of Change
- Direct variation
- Inverse variation
- Numerical sequences
- Algebraic expressions
- Algebraic equations

Mathematical Functions
- Models with real-world phenomena
- Forms of representations
  - Tables
  - Graphs
  - Function notation
- Relationships (between variable quantities)
- Properties of graphs
  - Intercepts
  - Slopes
  - Maximum/Minimum
  - Rates of change
  - Changes in rates of change

Methods of Solution
- Numerical
- Graphical
- Symbolical

Real-World Application
- Equations
- Expressions
- Inequalities

Skills: **Be Able to <u>Do</u>**

- Recognize (variety of math and real-world phenomena)
- Describe (relationships among variable quantities)
- Use (math functions in a variety of ways; appropriate technology)
- Represent/Model (with algebraic expressions, equations, inequalities)

[8] Reprinted with permission.

(continued)

- Solve
  - Inequalities and quadratic equations
  - Linear inequalities
  - Systems of linear equalities and inequalities
- Interpret (properties of graphical representations)
- Analyze/Generalize (patterns of change, numerical sequences)

Topics or Context:

- Lessons and activities to impart understanding of how to use mathematical functions in a variety of ways, along with the correct use of appropriate technology

Big Ideas

1. Algebra can be used to model real-world problems.

2. Mathematical and real-world problems can be solved using a variety of methods.

3. There are many different representations of mathematical functions.

Essential Questions

1. What is a mathematical model? How can algebra be used to solve real-world problems?

2. What methods can be used to mathematically represent real-world problems?

3. How many ways are there to solve a mathematical formula?

SCIENCE—Ecology
Grade 9
David Nagel and Kevin Self[9]
South Wayne Junior High
MSD Wayne Township
Indianapolis, Indiana

Concepts: **Need to <u>Know</u> About <u>Ecology</u>**

Environmental Cycles
- Carbon
- Oxygen
- Nitrogen

Ecosystems
- Types of biomes

Negative Effects on Environments
- Pollution
- Greenhouse effect
- Deforestation
- Overpopulation
- Acid rain
- Recycling

Predator/Prey Relationship

Food Chains/Food Webs

Succession/Biodiversity

Natural Selection

Skills: **Be Able to <u>Do</u>**

- Explain (environmental cycles, negative effects on environment, natural selection)
- Recognize (food chains, food webs, predator/prey relationships, negative effects on environments, ecosystems)
- Understand (predator/prey relationships, succession/biodiversity, natural selection)
- Describe (environmental cycles, ecosystems, negative effects on environments, predator/prey relationships, natural selection)
- Realize (negative effects on environment)

Topics or Context:

- Ecology unit

(continued)

Big Ideas

1. All living things are affected by living and nonliving factors within the environment.

2. Environmental factors influence the success of an ecosystem (abiotic and biotic).

3. All living matter and energy flow through an ecosystem and are recycled for the continuance of life.

4. Complex systems must maintain a balanced equilibrium in order for all organisms within them to exist.

5. Changes can cause dramatic shifts in organisms or environment.

Essential Questions

1. What role do the living and nonliving factors within an environment play on living things?

2. How do human activities negatively affect the environment?

3. What are the major players within the "Cycle of Life"? How do the major players interact?

4. How can a change from a state of equilibrium affect an ecosystem?

PHYSICAL SCIENCE
Grade 9
Teresa Haga, Glen Fromwiller, and Peter A'Hearn[10]
Desert Hot Springs High School and Palm Springs High School
Palm Springs Unified School District
Palm Springs, California

Concepts: ***Need to <u>Know</u> About <u>Physical Science</u>***

Tools and technology

Newton's second law

Newton's third law

Kinetic energy

Gravitational potential energy

Skills: ***Be Able to <u>Do</u>***

- Select
- Use
- Perform
- Collect
- Analyze
- Display
- Solve
- Apply
- Calculate
- Design
- Reflect
- Evaluate

Topics or Context:

- Forces and Energy lessons and activities

Big Ideas

1. Experimental results can be used to create models for describing the natural world.

2. The motion of objects can be approximated by using Newton's laws.

3. The energy of an object is related to its mass, velocity, and height.

Essential Questions

1. How does science attempt to describe the natural world?

2. How can we understand the motion of objects?

3. How can we calculate the energy of an object?

[10] Reprinted with permission.

EARTH SCIENCE
Grades 9–12
Anonymous

Concepts: *Need to <u>Know</u> About <u>Our Solar System</u>*

Sun and Planets
- The sun
- Terrestrial planets
- Gas planets

Solar Systems
- Earth and moon rocks
- Nebular cloud

Earth
- Geological studies
- Early Earth/Earth today

Scale
- Planets
- Stars

Sun
- A star
- Nuclear reaction
- Hydrogen and helium

Impact of Asteroids
- Life on earth
- Surface of planets/moons

Planets
- Other stars

Skills: *Be Able to <u>Do</u>*
- Describe (our solar system)
- Analyze (characteristics of the components)
- Distinguish (similarities and differences)
- Categorize (similar objects)
- Predict (future state, possible changes)

Topics or Context:
- Solar System Unit

Big Ideas

1. A solar system is made up of a star and all of its orbiting objects.
2. Our solar system was formed from a cloud of dust and gas.
3. Parts of our solar system are constantly interacting with one another.
4. Our solar system is constantly evolving.

Essential Questions

1. What is a solar system? How was our solar system formed
2. What changes are taking place in our solar system?

CHEMISTRY
Grades 11–12
Mark Fife, Bonnie Buddendeck, and Emily Erwin[11]
Centerville High School
Centerville, Ohio

Concepts: ***Need to <u>Know</u> About <u>Chemistry</u>***

Chemical Basis of Periodic Table
- Periodic trends
- Metals and non-metals
- Atomic structure
- Writing equations
- Physical and chemical properties
- The MOLE

Natural Resources
- Definitions
- Identifications
- Nonrenewable and renewable
- Conservation
- Uses
- Locations where they are found

Human Activity
- Usages of natural resources
- Trends of usage
- Mining
- Recyclable materials
- Advanced technology for substitution

Skills: ***Be Able to <u>Do</u>***

- Construct
- Analyze
- Observe
- Predict
- Conclude
- Communicate
- Compare/contrast

Topics or Context:

- Natural Resources Unit

---

[11] Reprinted with permission.   *(continued)*

Big Ideas

1. Resources are either renewable or nonrenewable.

2. Humans contribute to the diminishing of natural resources.

3. Chemical composition affects the properties of natural resources.

Essential Questions

1. Are we *really* running out of natural resources?

2. How do humans impact the availability of natural resources?

3. How does chemical composition determine which elements should be used as resources?

4. What types of substitutes could be developed to preserve our natural resources?

HISTORY/SOCIAL SCIENCE
Grade 10
Teresa Hudock[12]
University of Southern California
Los Angeles, California

Concepts: ***Need to <u>Know</u> About <u>Post WWII International</u> <u>Developments</u>—Cold War (1945–1990)***
California Standard 10.9

	Actors	Conditions/Events (cases)

POLITICAL	*Superpowers*
	  United States
	  Soviet Union (USSR)
	Soviet client states
	  Eastern Europe
	  satellites, bloc
	China → PRC/ROC
	
	United Nations
	OAS
		Cold War, *balance of power*
		  Truman Doctrine, *containment*
		  communism → collapse/*dissolution*
		
		uprisings: Poland, Hungary,
		  Czechoslovakia
		Chinese Civil War → Cultural
		  Revolution → Tiananmen Square
		
		Nationalism ← *decolonization*
		Holocaust → Israel/Middle East

MILITARY	NATO WARSAW PACT SEATO	competition for influence → *arms race* nuclear weapons, *MAD* → *loose nukes* Yalta Pact, Korean War Vietnam War → *Vietnam today* Cuba → *Cuba today* Egypt, the Congo, Chile
ECONOMIC	Germany and Japan China (PRC)	Marshall Plan → *Afghanistan* Great Leap Forward

Note: Text in italics were not specifically stated in the standard.

Skills: **Be Able to <u>Do</u>**

- Describe (actors and events)
- Understand (Cold War)
- Analyze (causes, importance)
- *Evaluate (relevant historical roots in today's world)

Topics or Context:

- Political history survey 1945 to 1990—current connections?

[12] Reprinted with permission.

Big Ideas

1. A shift in the global balance of power creates different dynamics between nations.

2. Technology impacts the effectiveness of weapons, military strategies, and security policies.

   The advent of nuclear weapons was a turning point in the history of humankind.

3. Not everybody learns the same lessons of history.

4. Security is not simply a military issue.

Essential Questions

1. How were the power shifts caused by the end of WWII similar to or different from the power shifts that are with us today caused by the end of the Cold War? How would you describe the current balance of power?

2. How is the effectiveness of a weapon affected by issues of strategy or circumstance? How is the role of nuclear weapons during the Cold War different or similar from the issues of nuclear weapons today?

3. As a turning point for U.S. security policy, what should be new directions in the post-Cold War era for current and future foreign policy decisions?

4. What is your perspective on how security can best be maintained today?

HISTORY/SOCIAL SCIENCE
Grade 10
Curt Greeley[13]
Righetti High School
Santa Maria Joint Union High School District
Santa Maria, California

Concepts:

Need to <u>Know</u> About <u>Glorious Revolution, American Revolution, and French Revolution</u>
California History Standard 10.2

- Major philosophers (Montesquieu, Locke, etc.)
  - Impact of their ideas
  - Effects on revolutions and government
- Uniqueness of American revolution
  - Impact and influence on other nations
- France's development
  - From despotism to constitutional monarchy through revolution
- Impact of nationalism in Europe
  - Growth under Napoleon
  - Its repression under Congress of Vienna (1848)

Skills:

Be Able to <u>Do</u>

- Compare
- Contrast
- Understand
- Discuss

Topics or Context:

- Debate governmental models forwarded by Enlightenment thinkers
- Examine American Revolution
- In-class simulation of French Revolution
- Reproduction of nationalistic emotions (examine pros and cons)

Big Idea

1. Revolutions have worldwide impact on political expectations for self-government and individual liberty.

Essential Questions

1. How did the Enlightenment philosophers directly contribute to revolution as an instrument for political change?

2. How did unhappiness with political and economic conditions in various western nations lead to revolutions in Europe, North America, and South America?

3. Why and how does such unhappiness provide a pattern for political change through revolution in emerging democracies?

[13] Reprinted with permission.

HISTORY/SOCIAL SCIENCE
Grade 11
Anonymous

Concepts:

Need to <u>Know</u> About <u>Post-WWII Foreign Policy</u>
California Standard 11.9

International Organizations
- Economy/trade
- Military/strategic
- Human rights/peace

Consequences
- Domestic
- Foreign
- Victory of the West

Post-Cold War Relations
- Middle East
- Mexico

Skills:

Be Able to <u>Do</u>
- List and describe
- Trace and discuss
- Examine
- Analyze

Topics or Context:

- United Nations
- Declaration of Human Rights
- IMF
- World Bank
- GATT
- NATO
- SEATO
- Containment
- McCarthyism
- Communism
- Truman Doctrine
- Berlin Blockade
- Korean War
- Bay of Pigs
- Cuban Missile Crisis
- "MAD"
- Vietnam
- Latin American policy
- "Nuclear Freeze"
- Gulf War
- Immigration

(continued)

Big Ideas

1. International military, economic, and social organizations shaped U.S. foreign policy after World War II.

2. Nations often work together to overcome international challenges.

3. A large, powerful country can dominate smaller countries all over the world.

4. Foreign policies connect and affect all nations.

Essential Questions

1. How was post-World War II policy shaped?

2. How do the political, economic, and social structures of differing nations connect?

3. How has U.S. foreign policy affected other nations?

4. How does the international community respond to worldwide challenges?

UNITED STATES HISTORY
Grade 11
Jason Smith[14]
Loara High School
Anaheim Union High School District
Anaheim, California

Concepts:

Need to <u>Know</u> About <u>THE GREAT DEPRESSION</u>

Politics
1. Steps taken by Congress to combat the Depression
2. Steps taken by the presidents to combat the Depression
3. Movements to the right and left
4. Expanded role of the federal government

Economics
1. Causes of the Great Depression
2. New Deal economic policies
3. Effect of the Okies and Arkies on the economy of California

Geography
1. Natural disasters—Dust Bowl
2. Depopulation of rural regions—theme of movement

Social
1. Human toll of the Depression
2. Effects of the Okies and Arkies in California

Skills:

Be Able to <u>Do</u>

- Discuss
- Understand
- Analyze

Topics or Context:

- Causes of the Great Depression
- Impact of the Great Depression on the American people
- The philosophies and the attempts made to end the Great Depression in the United States

[14] Reprinted with permission.

(continued)

Big Ideas

1. The Great Depression caused enduring changes in the role of the federal government in the daily lives of the American people.

2. The interwoven nature of the American economic system affects all social groups in both prosperous and declining periods.

Essential Questions

1. How did the role of the government in the daily lives of Americans change during the Great Depression? Why did it change?

2. Have the changes in governmental philosophy endured until today? What are some examples?

3. How do economic slowdowns and times of prosperity affect all Americans?

GOVERNMENT
Grade 12
Larry Lawson[15]
Ben Davis High School
MSD Wayne Township
Indianapolis, Indiana

Concepts: | *Need to <u>Know</u> About <u>Citizenship, Politics, and Government</u>*

I. Structures
   A. Government
      1. Purpose
      2. Function
   B. Politics
      1. Ideologies
      2. Democracy

II. Systems
   A. Comparative
      1. Forms of government
      2. Kinds of democracy
      3. History of authority
   B. Legal
      1. History of law
      2. Constitutionalism

III. Participation
   A. Civic Life
      1. Maintenance of
         a. Limited government
         b. Democracy
   B. Political Life
      1. Interaction of citizens and government
      2. Individual rights
   C. Private Life
      1. Feelings

Skills: | *Be Able to <u>Do</u>*

1. Compare and Contrast
2. Distinguish
   a. Describe
   b. Examine
3. Analyze
4. Identify and Define

[15] Reprinted with permission.

(continued)

Big Ideas

I. Structure
    A. Democracy has developed from many forms of government.

II. Systems
    A. The history of law evolved in ways that made democracy possible.

III. Participation
    A. Citizens' participation in their political affairs has had a positive effect upon their lives.

Essential Questions

I. Structure
    A. Why do we choose to have a democratic form of government?

II. Systems
    A. What effect has the development of law had on democracy?

III. Participation
    A. How would your participation in government help to continue our democracy?

FOREIGN LANGUAGE—Spanish
Grade 9
Laura McMillan, Marianna Aguirre, Alejandra Munoz, and Victoria Geibig[16]
Tracy Unified School District
Tracy, California

Concepts:

Need to <u>Know</u> About <u>Spanish Level 1</u>

Communicating in the Target Language,
Standards 1.1, 1.2, 3.1, 4.1, 4.2

Communication (1.1, 1.2)
- Conversations
- Information
- Feelings and emotions
- Opinions

Culture (4.2)
- Understanding
- Comparisons

Grammar (3.1)
- Knowledge
- Disciplines
- Foreign language

Vocabulary (4.1)
- Nature of language
- Own language
- Language studied
- Comparisons

Skills:

Be Able to <u>Do</u> (Organized by Concepts)

Communication
- Engage (in conversations)
- Provide (information)
- Obtain (information)
- Express (feelings and emotions)
- Exchange (opinions)
- Understand (written and spoken language)
- Interpret (written and spoken language)

Grammar
- Reinforce and further (knowledge)

Vocabulary
- Demonstrate (understanding)

Culture
- Demonstrate (understanding of concept of culture)

[16] Reprinted with permission.

(continued)

FOREIGN LANGUAGE—Spanish
Grade 9, Laura McMillan, Marianna Aguirre, Alejandra Munoz, and Victoria Geibig,
Tracy Unified School District, Tracy, California *(continued)*

Topics or Context:

- Variety of topics using conversation
- Textbook
- Workbook and worksheets
- Videos
- Group work
- Dialogues
- Skits
- Writing activities

Big Ideas

1. Knowing another language can help you communicate in other cultures.

2. A broad vocabulary helps you get your point across effectively.

3. Understanding of grammar helps to communicate with others.

4. Knowing about other cultures helps to understand other ethnicities and to break down stereotypes.

Essential Questions

1. Why is it important to learn another language?

2. Why are so many words needed to say one thing?

3. Why do I need to learn grammar?

4. Why do I have to learn about other cultures and people?

COMPUTER APPLICATIONS — PowerPoint Presentations
John Crum and Andy Kennedy[17]
Ben Davis High School
MSD Wayne Township
Indianapolis, Indiana

Concepts: ***Need to <u>Know</u> About <u>PowerPoint Presentations</u>***
Indiana Computer Applications Standard 4 High School

Simple Presentations
- Purpose
- Different types of presentation software
- Basic presentation terminology
- Basic principles of design
- Editing functions
- Slides/cards in various formats

Advanced Enhancement Features
- Terminology (layouts, templates, text, objects, color, bullets, page numbers, drawings, animations, video, sounds, graphs, tables, and charts)
- Advanced principles of visual design

Software Application Documents
- Terminology associated with software integration
- Spreadsheet, word processing, database files

Refinement and Delivery
- Terminology (transitions, effects, timings, annotations)
- Outline view and notes pages view
- Proper public speaking techniques

Skills: ***Be Able to <u>Do</u>***

- Define and apply (terminology, principles of design)
- Create, save, print (basic presentation)
- Explain (purpose of different types of presentations)
- Utilize (editing functions)
- Save and print (slide cards in various formats)
- Apply (advanced principles of visual design)
- Integrate (software application documents)
- Import and link (spreadsheet, word-processing, database)
- Refine and deliver (presentation)
- Modify (presentation with layouts, color, etc.)

[17] Reprinted with permission.

(continued)

- Enhance (presentation with advanced features)
- Use (multiple views, editing functions)
- Research (Internet)
- Utilize (outline view, notes pages, public speaking techniques)

Topics or Context:

- Microsoft PowerPoint Unit
- Real-life applications

Big Ideas

1. Knowledge and application of PowerPoint terms are necessary for presentation design.

2. The visual design of a presentation is important to display a clear message.

3. Enhancing presentations adds emphasis to key points or concepts.

4. Public speaking skills are an essential part of every presentation.

Essential Questions

1. What are the requirements of effective visual presentations?

2. Why is visual design important to a presentation?

3. How do you add emphasis to key points or concepts?

4. Technology aside, what enhances a PowerPoint presentation?

CAREER AND BUSINESS EDUCATION
Grades 9–12
Deborah Laughlin and Kim Plunkett[18]
Career Education
Centerville High School
Centerville, Ohio

Concepts:	***Need to <u>Know</u> About <u>Planning and Managing a Career</u>***

Seeking a Career
- Interests, abilities, aptitudes, and skills
- Strategies, techniques, and information
  - For getting a job/career
  - For maintaining a job/career

Skills:	***Be Able to <u>Do</u>***

- Identify (interests, abilities, aptitudes, skills)
- Conduct (job search)
- Write (cover letter and resume)
- Fill out (job application)
- Communicate (human relations skills)
- Manage (time)
- Pursue (lifelong learning)

Topics or Context:

- Material on "Career Goals"
- Material on "Employability Skills"
- Material on "Maintaining the Career"
- Discover
- OCIS
- Internet

Big Ideas

1. Individuals examine their aptitudes, interests, skills, and abilities when applying for a job.
2. Individuals need time management skills to maintain a job/career.
3. Individuals use technology to search for possible careers.
4. Individuals who obtain and keep employment develop and continually refine their ability to work collaboratively with others.

Essential Questions

1. What do individuals need to consider when seeking a job or career?
2. What are the necessary skills for maintaining a job or career?
3. Where can individuals obtain information about career opportunities?
4. What are the communication skills needed for successful employment? How can they be acquired?

[18] Reprinted with permission.

CAREER AND BUSINESS EDUCATION
Grades 9–12
Amy Lange and Diane Voit[19]
West and North High Schools
School District of Waukesha
Waukesha, Wisconsin

Concepts:

Need to Know About Effective Meeting Procedures
Representing Language Arts, Business Education, and
Marketing Education Standards and Indicators

Discussions
- Roles (leader, participant, moderator)
- Audience/Participants (motivation, bias)
- Relevant information (accuracy, usefulness, source, fact vs. opinion, logic, validity, manipulative techniques)
- Pertinent questions
- Persuasive messages
- Summaries (main ideas, areas of agreement, conclusions)
- Problem solving
- Conflict resolution (negotiation skills)
- Proper etiquette (listening, consideration, respect, responses, feedback)

Meetings
- Agenda
- Parliamentary Procedure
- Communication Skills (eye contact, inflection, enunciation)
- Minutes

Skills:

Be Able to Do

Demonstrate
- Various discussion roles
- Question-and-answer techniques
- Persuasion
- Problem solving
- Conflict resolution
- Effective parliamentary procedure
- Proper etiquette

Analyze
- Information

Evaluate
- Participant discussion

[19] Reprinted with permission.

(continued)

CAREER AND BUSINESS EDUCATION
Grades 9 –12, **Amy Lange and Diane Voit,** West and North High Schools,
School District of Waukesha, Waukesha, Wisconsin *(continued)*

Formulate
- Questions
- Appropriate responses

Summarize
- Main ideas (agenda)
- Areas of agreement
- Conclusions
- Written record (minutes)

Topics or Context:

- Meeting Etiquette
- Parliamentary Procedure
- Persuasive Techniques

Big Ideas

1. Effective leaders can influence decisions.

2. An agenda is the road map to getting things done.

3. Parliamentary procedure describes the "rules of the road" at a meeting.

4. What you say and how you say it can get results.

Essential Questions

1. What traits do effective leaders share? Why do those traits make them successful?

2. How can meeting time be made more productive?

3. What are the basics of parliamentary procedure? How can parliamentary procedure help to accomplish outcomes?

4. How can you get the results you want in a meeting?

VISUAL ARTS
Grade 9
Dawn Adams, Jon Wesney, and Jennifer Moore[20]
Centerville High School
Centerville, Ohio

Concepts:　　　　***Need to <u>Know</u> About <u>Ceramics and 3-D Art</u>***

Elements/Principles
- Line
- Texture
- Color
- Shape/Form
- Unity
- Variety
- Proportion
- Repetition

Processes
- Wedging
- Wheel-thrown
- Hand-building
  - Coil
  - Slab
  - Pinch

History
- Religious
- Decorative
- Economic
- Political

Media
- Clay
- Glaze
- Tools

Skills:　　　　***Be Able to <u>Do</u>***

- Understand
- Compare/contrast
- Identify
- Apply
- Create
- Communicate

---

[20] Reprinted with permission.

(continued)

VISUAL ARTS

Grade 9, **Dawn Adams, Jon Wesney, and Jennifer Moore,** Centerville High School, Centerville, Ohio *(continued)*

Topics or Context:

- Slides of history
- Videos of artists
- Examples
- Models
- Demonstrations

Big Ideas

1. Ceramics has played a significant part in the development of civilization.

2. Knowledge and application of the principles of ceramic construction are needed to produce a piece of pottery.

3. Visual artists must understand how the elements and principles of art apply to a 3-D art form.

Essential Questions

1. Why is the study of ceramics important?

2. What goes into the production of a quality piece of pottery?

3. What art elements and principles apply to ceramic construction?

PERFORMING ARTS—Music
Grades 9–12
Darien Martus, Brian Ingelson, Patricia Reed, and Michael Bukraba[21]
Palm Springs Unified School District
Palm Springs, California

Targeted Standard(s): Standard 1 Artistic Perception (1.6)

Standard 2 Creative Expression (2.1–2.5)

Standard 3 Historical and Cultural Context (3.1–3.5)

Standard 4 Aesthetic Valuing (4.1–4.4)

Standard 5 Connections, Relationships, Applications (5.1–5.3)

Concepts:

Need to __Know__ About __PERFORMANCE SKILLS__

Varied repertoire of music representing various genres, styles, and cultures

Vocal and/or instrumental technique
- Tone
- Rhythm
- Key signature
- Articulation
- Technical accuracy

Rehearsal technique and expectations

Skills:

Be Able to __Do__
- Perform (instrumental or vocal selection by oneself and with an ensemble)
- Apply (rehearsal technique and expectations)

Topics or Context:
- Performance skills

Big Ideas

1. Music performance can be attained through understanding of instrumental and vocal study.
2. Music performance incorporates a variety of literature from various genres, styles, and cultures.
3. Music performance is attained through implementation of instrumental or vocal technique.

Essential Questions

1. How do you apply instrumental or vocal study to musical performance?
2. How do you perform using literature from various genres, styles, and culture?
3. How do you perform?

[21] Reprinted with permission.

CULINARY ARTS & HOSPITALITY—Food Service Industry
Grades 11–12
Linda Valiga[22]
Waukesha South High School
School District of Waukesha
Waukesha, Wisconsin

Concepts:

Need to <u>Know</u> About <u>Food Safety and Sanitation</u>
Wisconsin Standards A3, B1, B4, C3, E2, E3

- Food Safety History
  - National and local
- Kinds of Bacteria
  - Harmless, beneficial, undesirable, and disease-causing
- Bacterial Growth
  - Conditions for growth—food, acidity, time, temperature, oxygen, moisture (FATTOM), locomotion
- Protection against Bacteria
- Food-Borne Diseases
  - Bacterial diseases, other food infections, chemical food poisoning
- Personal Hygiene
- Setting up a Food Safety System—Hazard Analysis Critical Control Points (HACCP)
  - Food storage: Dry, freezer, refrigerator, holding of hot foods
  - Food handling and preparation
  - Cleaning and sanitizing: Cleaning schedules, recycling

Skills:

Be Able to <u>Do</u>

- Know HACCP (Hazard Analysis Critical Control Points)
  - Kinds of food-borne illness
  - Flow of food
  - FATTOM (Food, acidity, time, temperature, oxygen, moisture)
  - Government agencies regulating food
- Understand (food safety history, kinds of bacteria, bacterial growth, protection against bacteria)

---

[22] Reprinted with permission.

(continued)

- Apply (flow of food, personal hygiene)
- Recognize and respond (risk factors in humans, symptoms of food-borne illnesses, errors in HACCP)
- Formulate (a HACCP plan for a lab)
- Model (food service safety standards, HACCP in a lab setting, usage of thermometers)
- Evaluate (real-world food safety situations)

Topics or Context:

- Job skills
- Applied microbiology in a real-world setting

Big Ideas

1. All food service establishments share a common concern/goal of serving safe food.

2. Good sanitation involves solutions to problems in a food-related setting.

3. Following proper food safety procedures (receiving, storing, preparing, cooking, holding, cooling, and reheating) will prevent food-borne illnesses.

4. A well-designed kitchen environment should be sanitary and clean.

5. Food service establishments should use HACCP (Hazard Analysis Critical Control Points) procedures to prevent food-borne illnesses.

Essential Questions

1. What food service procedures need to be followed to prevent food-borne illnesses?

2. What is the difference between clean and sanitary?

3. What are the proper procedures for cleaning and sanitizing equipment?

4. What are the steps in HACCP, and why are they important in operating a food service establishment?

5. What is FATTOM, and why is it critical in serving safe food?

Gary Moore, Jolene Azevedo, Chelsea Stephens, and Chuck Selna[23]
Tracy Unified School District
Tracy, California

Concepts: ***Need to <u>Know</u> About <u>Fitness</u>***
District P.E. Standard(s): 2.1.1, 2.1.2, 2.1.3

Positive Self-Image:
- Self-Esteem
- Self-Respect
- Confidence
- Body Composition

Individual Fitness Program
- Target Heart Rate
- Aerobic/Anaerobic Exercise
- Stretching
- Stress Level
- Weight Training
- Time and Frequency
- Personal Goals
- Sports Interests

Skills: ***Be Able to <u>Do</u>***

- Demonstrate (skills to reduce stress)
- Demonstrate (problem-solving skills in group setting)
- Demonstrate (cooperation, acceptance, and belonging within a group or team activity)
- Understand (Heart Rate Zone)
- Find (Target Heart Rate)
- Understand (difference between aerobic and anaerobic activity)
- Compose (obtainable goals for personal and physical fitness)
- Identify (sports-specific muscle groups)
- Recognize (general concepts of sports)

Topics or Context:

- Fitness unit
- Team cooperation unit
- Individual sports unit
- Team sports unit

[23] Reprinted with permission.

(continued)

Big Ideas

1. No matter the amount of stress in your environment, always strive to obtain the best for yourself.

2. Show respect for all students regardless of personal differences or fitness levels so cultural and physical barriers break down.

3. It is necessary to participate in physical activity to maintain a healthy lifestyle.

4. Working out properly guarantees that maximum potential and benefits are met.

Essential Questions

1. What are some things that affect the way we feel about ourselves? How do we overcome them?

2. What does respect look like?

3. Why should you be physically active?

4. What does working out mean to you? How does it help you?

CHAPTER NINE

"Unwrapping" the Standards— The Step-by-Step Process

The purpose of this chapter is to provide a summary of the steps to follow when "unwrapping" standards and indicators, determining Big Ideas, and writing Essential Questions. My intent is to present this series of steps, repeated from preceding chapters without the explanatory commentary, in a checklist format for easy reference by educators working through the "unwrapping' process. If any step below is not fully understandable, please refer back to the corresponding chapter for further explanation.

The "Unwrapping" Standards Process

Chapter One: "Unwrapping" the Standards

❑ Present rationale for "unwrapping" standards

❑ Define terms:
   - "Unwrapping" (finding the concepts and skills in standards wording)
   - Concepts (important nouns—what students need to know)
   - Skills (verbs—what students need to be able to do)
   - Topics or Context (lessons and activities used to teach concepts and skills)
   - Big Ideas (lasting understandings students determine on their own)
   - Essential Questions (posed at beginning of unit to guide instruction and assessment)

❑ Select standards and related indicators to "unwrap"

❑ Underline important nouns (concepts) and circle verbs (skills)

❑ Create graphic organizer of choice (bulleted list, outline, concept map)
   - List concepts individually or group related ones under headings
   - List skills in same sequence as they appear in standards OR list by Bloom's *Taxonomy* order
   - List target of each skill parenthetically
     ○ Example: Demonstrate (cause and effect)

❑ Decide topics or context (lessons or activities to teach concepts and skills)

❑ If "unwrapping" same standard with colleague(s):
   - Compare graphic organizers
   - Note whether same elements appear even though format may be different

❏ Double-check that all important concepts and skills are represented on graphic organizer so standards can be "put aside" in confidence

Chapter Two: Finding the Big Ideas

❏ Present rationale for identifying Big Ideas

❏ Define Big Ideas:
- "Aha!" or "lightbulb" insights
- Lasting understandings students make *on their own* after instruction
- New connections students make to what they already know
- Student answers to *teacher's* Essential Questions

❏ Attributes of Big Ideas:
- Brief
- Conceptual
- Open-ended
- Enduring

❏ Guidelines for determining each Big Idea:
- Applies to more than one area of learning
- Appears in other grade levels
- Stands "test of time"; will remain important to know
- Memorable long after instruction ends

❏ Use graphic organizer to identify Big Ideas:
- Move from concrete (represented concepts and skills) to abstract (Big Ideas)
- Ask: "What do I want students to realize on *their own* after I finish teaching them these concepts and skills?"
- Write three or four Big Ideas from represented concepts and skills
- Can be topical (apply to one content area) or broad (apply to several content areas)
- If difficult to identify:
  ○ Determine one Big Idea for each concept heading on graphic organizer
  ○ Refer to standards *Introduction* section for broader learning goals (often similar to Big Ideas)
  ○ Collaborate with another colleague
- Write in student-friendly language: simple, conversational

Chapter Three: Writing the Essential Questions

❏ Present rationale for writing Essential Questions

❏ Define Essential Questions:
- Standards-based
- Succinct, open-ended, cannot be answered with "yes," "no," or mere recall of facts only
- Require higher-level thinking skill responses
- Announced at beginning of instruction as the learning goals
- *Not* restatements of the Big Ideas—the "hooks" to engage learners
- Resulting student work provides evidence that standards are met
- Can be *topical* (reflect specific learning outcomes) or *broad* (applicable to more than one content area)

❑ Review Big Ideas

❑ Write Essential Questions that will lead students to same Big Ideas

❑ Evaluate Essential Questions:
  – Represent concepts and skills from "unwrapped" standards?
  – One-two punch questions: content knowledge + higher-level thinking?
  – Big Ideas *answer* the Essential Questions?
  – Could be posted in classroom at beginning of unit to guide instruction and assessment?
  – Could be used for summative assessment?

This is by no means an all-inclusive checklist of every consideration that goes through the mind of an educator who is "unwrapping" the state standards and then determining Big Ideas and Essential Questions. But it will provide a "snapshot" of the necessary steps to follow when beginning and working through the process *and* when sharing this process with others. As educators become more and more familiar with the steps involved, they will have mastered a relatively simple yet truly effective method for managing the standards!

CHAPTER TEN

From "Unwrapping" Standards to Performance Assessments

"Unwrapping" Is the First Step

At the conclusion of a one-day "unwrapping" standards seminar I conducted for the department chairpersons of a high school in the Midwest, one of the participants stopped to thank me as he was leaving.

"It was great to learn something that I can actually use," he said.

"I'm glad. I know how important it is for professional development to be relevant and practical," I replied.

"The 'unwrapping' will better focus my instruction, and the Big Ideas will remind me to emphasize higher-order thinking skills. I've got the whole picture now. Thanks again."

He shook my hand and moved toward the door.

I said enthusiastically, "You know, there's another step beyond this. After you 'unwrap' the standards, you can design performance assessment tasks to help your students learn the 'unwrapped' concepts and answer the Essential Questions with their own Big Ideas!"

His reply surprised me, but it held its own logic.

"Don't tell me about anything else right now, okay? I just want to do what you showed us today. This alone is enough to really improve my teaching."

I smiled and said, "Point taken. We'll save that for next time."

"Unwrapping" Standards: A Part of the Whole

In The Leadership and Learning Center's professional development seminar, *Making Standards Work,* named after Dr. Douglas B. Reeves's pioneering book by the same title (1996), educators work collaboratively to design a standards-based performance assessment. The design steps of Dr. Reeves's performance assessment model include:

1. Targeting standards and indicators within one content area.

2. Making interdisciplinary connections by identifying related standards and indicators in *other* content areas.

3. Creating an Engaging Scenario to "hook" student interest.

4. Designing a collection of several related performance tasks that enable students to develop their understanding of the targeted standards and indicators.

5. Writing task-specific scoring guides or rubrics to evaluate the degree of proficiency in the work that students produce.

After developing the "unwrapping" standards process, I expanded the five components above and then rearranged the sequence of design steps so that the model now looks like this:

1. Target standards and indicators in one content area.

2. "Unwrap" those standards and indicators; create a graphic organizer.

3. Identify the Big Ideas.

4. Write the Essential Questions.

5. Design performance tasks based on the "unwrapped" standard(s) and indicators.

6. Identify *interdisciplinary* standards and indicators reflected in performance tasks.

7. Create an Engaging Scenario to introduce and link performance tasks.

8. Develop scoring guides or rubrics to assess the performance tasks.

Typically, the seminar is conducted over three days. On the first day, participants complete steps one through four. On the second day, they complete steps five through seven. On the final day, they complete step eight and leave the seminar with a first draft of an "unwrapped" standards-based performance assessment ready to use in their own instructional programs.

Individual schools and entire school systems have a limited number of hours and days available each year for professional development. If three *consecutive* days are not available to complete all the components of the performance assessment model, participants begin with the one-day seminar on "unwrapping." They can immediately implement that part of the process in their own programs and then return days, weeks, or even months later to complete the remaining components of the performance assessment model.

"Unwrapping" *Power* Standards

The three-day seminar begins with the rationale and overview of the process for identifying Power Standards, a way to *prioritize* the standards and thus identify a subset of all the standards in each content area that educators decide are the most critical for student success—in school each year, in life, and on all high-stakes assessment measures. Participants learn how to select the standards and indicators they believe are most critical for student success in their individual grades and/or departments. They then "unwrap" those Power Standards to identify the important concepts and skills contained within them. The full explanation of the rationale and process for identifying Power Standards can be found in the *"Unwrapping" the Standards* companion volume, *Power Standards* (Ainsworth, 2003).

In Conclusion

A good idea, poorly implemented, is a bad idea! Therefore, I advocate introducing new professional practices one at a time and implementing each one effectively *before* introducing the next new practice.

The process of "unwrapping" the standards provides educators with a simple yet highly effective way to manage the standards. Whether or not educators have yet designed and used standards-based performance assessments in their own instructional programs, "unwrapping" the standards will provide them with a first step to better focus instruction on the concepts and skills students need for success. They can then draw upon their own teaching talents and expertise in order to help students grasp the Big Ideas and answer the Essential Questions. They can design their own assessments that afford students the opportunity to "show all they know" with regard to the "unwrapped" concepts, skills, and Big Ideas. The resulting improvements in student achievement that K-12 educators are sure to witness will motivate them to say, "This really worked! What else can I do?" And that may be the appropriate time to introduce them to the remaining steps in the performance assessment design model.

It is my hope that educators will share the "unwrapping" standards process with colleagues, review with one another the grade-span examples that were provided throughout these pages, apply the process first and foremost in their own instructional programs, compare and contrast the results, and then plan for the further implementation of the "unwrapping" process throughout the grades, departments, schools, and entire district!

Contact Information

If you have any additional questions as you work through the "unwrapping" standards process, or should you wish to share your own feedback after implementing these ideas, please do not hesitate to contact my colleagues or me at The Leadership and Learning Center. We welcome your ideas and are here to support you! Our contact information is listed below.

My best wishes as you make the "unwrapping" standards process your own!

Larry Ainsworth
Executive Director of Professional Development
The Leadership and Learning Center
(866) 399-6019, ext. 509
www.LeadandLearn.com

"Unwrapping" Standards Template

"Unwrapping" Content Standards

Grade Level and Content Area
Standard(s) and Indicators (Listed by Number Only):

<u>Concepts</u>: Need to <u>Know</u> About

<u>Skills</u>: Be Able to <u>Do</u>

<u>Topics or Context</u>: (What you will use to teach concepts and skills— particular unit, lessons, activities)

Identifying "Big Ideas" from "Unwrapped" Standard(s) and Indicators

1.

2.

3.

4.

Essential Questions from Big Ideas to Guide Instruction and Assessment

1.

2.

3.

4.

Bloom's *Taxonomy*[1]

Definitions

Verbs that express varying levels of understanding

Appropriate responses

1. **Knowledge — Remembering facts**
   Verbs: Know, define, memorize, record, name, recognize
   Describe _____.
   Who? What? Where? When? How?[2]

2. **Comprehension — Understanding the meaning**
   Verbs: Discuss, relate, clarify, explain
   Retell in your own words _____.
   What is the main idea of _____?

3. **Application — Using what you know in a new situation**
   Verbs: Translate, interpret, demonstrate, dramatize, practice
   Why is _____ significant?

4. **Analysis — Examining specific parts of information**
   Verbs: Distinguish, analyze, differentiate, solve, examine
   Classify _____ according to _____.
   Compare and contrast _____ and _____.

5. **Synthesis — Combing ideas in a new way**
   Verbs: Compose, plan, propose, formulate, arrange
   What could you predict from _____?
   What solutions would you suggest from _____?

6. **Evaluation — Developing opinions, judgments, or decisions**
   Verbs: Judge, appraise, evaluate, estimate, select
   Do you agree with _____?
   Prioritize _____.
   What is the most important _____?

[1] Bloom, 1956.

[2] Questions attributed to Mary Gifford.

References

Ainsworth, L. (2003). *Power standards: Identifying the standards that matter the most.* Denver: Lead + Learn Press.

Ainsworth, L. & Christinson, J. (1998). *Student-generated rubrics.* New York: Dale Seymour Publications.

Bloom, B.S. (Ed.). (1956). *Taxonomy of educational objectives: The classification of educational goals: Handbook I, cognitive domain.* New York: Longmans, Green.

Brady, M. (2000, May). "The standards juggernaut." *Phi Delta Kappan, 81*(9), 650.

Erickson, H. L. (2000). *Concept-based curriculum and instruction: Teaching beyond the facts.* Thousand Oaks, CA: Corwin Press.

Merrill Area Public Schools. (1999, April). *Curriculum: Providing a rich, purposeful plan for what students should know and be able to do.* Merrill, WI: Author.

Olson, L. (2002). "States anxious for federal guidance on yearly progress." *Education Week,* November 27, 2002, p. 15.

Reeves, D. B. (1996). *Making standards work*, 3d. Ed. (2002). Denver: Lead + Learn Press.

Traver, R. (1998, March). "What is a good guiding question?" *Educational Leadership, 55*(6), 70–73.

Wiggins, G. & McTighe, J. (1998). *Understanding by design.* Alexandria, VA: Association for Supervision and Curriculum Development.

Original Sources of Standards and Indicators Cited in Text

- First Example: Grade 2 Mathematics Standard — Kansas

- Second Example: Grade 5 Science Standard — Washington, D.C.

- Third Example: Grade 6 History/Social Science Standards — California

- World History and Geography — Ancient Civilizations *Introduction* — California

- Fourth Example: End of Grades 8–10, Writing Applications Benchmarks — Ohio

- Writing Applications, End of Grades 8–10 *Introduction* — Ohio

- Fifth Example: Grade 12 Reading Standard — Ohio (Prior to 2002 Revision)

Index

Resources for Improved Student Achievement
Other Books by Lead + Learn Press

Making Standards Work:
How to Implement Standards-Based Assessments in the Classroom, School, and District

By Douglas B. Reeves, Ph.D.

Performance assessments are powerful tools for accurately measuring what students know and are able to do. *Making Standards Work* leads you through the steps of creating and using performance assessments to determine your students' achievement throughout the school year. Dr. Reeves' straightforward approach to improving student achievement begins with using performance assessments that contain real-world scenarios, multiple tasks, and clear, consistent scoring guides. Thousands of educators have used this book as an essential guide to creating effective standards-based classrooms, schools, and districts.

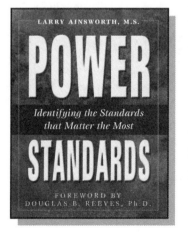

Power Standards:
Identifying the Standards that Matter the Most

By Larry Ainsworth

Power Standards presents a proven process for identifying the standards that matter the most, a process that can be used successfully with every state's standards in every content area and at every grade level. The book is designed to be a step-by-step, practical manual that educators can use immediately in their own districts to replicate the process others have successfully followed.

Do you believe all students can succeed?

Can educators make a difference and produce results?

So much to do and so little time!

Since 1992, school districts and educational organizations seeking to improve student achievement have consulted with The Leadership and Learning Center. Educational leaders on five continents have collaboratively created customized solutions based on research and results. If you would like to know more about the services of The Leadership and Learning Center, to learn about success stories in every type of educational setting, to find out about the latest research, or to arrange a presentation by a Center consultant, please visit the Web site at *www.LeadandLearn.com* or contact:

LEAD AND LEARN
Making A Difference...Today

317 Inverness Way South, Suite 150 ▪ Englewood, CO 80112
(866) 399-6019 ▪ Fax (303) 504-9417